D0375053

Get Over It!

**Thought Therapy
for Healing the
Hard Stuff**

Get Over It!

Thought Therapy for Healing the Hard Stuff

IYANLA Vanzant

Hay House, Inc.
Carlsbad, California • New York City
London • Sydney • Johannesburg
Vancouver • New Delhi

Published and distributed in the United States by: Hay House, Inc.: www.hayhouse
.com • **Published and distributed in Australia by:** Hay House Australia Pty. Ltd.:
www.hayhouse.com.au • **Published and distributed in the United Kingdom by:** Hay
House UK, Ltd.: www.hayhouse.co.uk • **Distributed in Canada by: Raincoast Books:**
www.raincoast.com • **Published and distributed in India by:** Hay House Publishers
India: www.hayhouse.co.in

Cover design: Kristine Mills-Noble
Interior design: Cindy Shaw / CreativeDetails.net

All quotes from *A Course in Miracles* are from the public domain edition, 1975.
Foundation for Inner Peace, P.O. Box 598, Mill Valley, 94942-0598, www.acim.org
and info@acim.org.

Library of Congress Control Number: 2017959583

Hardcover ISBN: 978-1-4019-4401-8

10 9 8 7 6 5 4 3
1st edition, January 2018

Printed in the United States of America

DEDICATION

✦

This book is dedicated to
the elder of the eldest grandmothers,
of all people, all races, and all nations,
who were the living embodiments of
grace and humility, demonstrating to the world
how to move through adversity with dignity

And . . .
the elder of the eldest grandfathers,
of all people, all races, and all nations,
who were living embodiments of commitment
to family and responsibility to community,
demonstrating to the world that manhood
is a condition of mind and being
that cannot be bought or sold.

I acknowledge you and call you
to an awakened state, to infuse the presence and
power of your lives into the conscious minds
of your descendants who are alive today.

Ache!
Hau Mitakuye Oyasin!

What you think means more

than anything else in your life —

more than what you earn,

more than where you live,

more than your social position,

and more than what anyone else

may think about you.

—George Matthew Adams

CONTENTS

✦

INTRODUCTION

✦

*"There is a light so intense, so powerful that
nothing other than itself can exist in its presence."*

"It is a light that never goes out."

*"Certainly, no lie or deception, no boundary or
defense can remain intact in its presence."*

"It is enduring power, and yet it is tender."

This light is natural.

When recognized, you do not think twice about it.

*You know that anything that "cannot stand
the heavenly heat" of this light "is to be
cast aside swiftly by conscious choice."*

This light is your soul's light.

The choice is yours to make.

IYANLA'S JOURNAL ENTRY
Incorporating lines from The Dissolving Light Card presented in the
Rumi Oracle: An Invitation into The Heart Of The Divine
by Alana Fairchild

ecause of the work I have done over the past
three decades and the increasingly dehumanizing
circumstances that have been normalized around the globe, I
am painfully aware that people of all genders, races, and ages,

and all political, social, and economic groups, are suffering at unprecedented levels. Many are suffering from psychological, emotional, and spiritual torment they do not understand, cannot seem to shake, or are unable to move beyond. Others are suffering because of habitual behaviors that motivate reckless decision-making and poor choices, keeping them stuck in repetitive cycles of dysfunction and despair.

For the purpose of the healing work that will be offered as the Get Over It! process, I am defining suffering in the following way: *"voluntary participation in situations and circumstances that diminish one's capacity and potential to thrive or flourish as a function of a belief that one is powerless to do anything else."*

The *Reader's Digest* definition of suffering would be this: There are those who suffer from crippling fears about the future. Mentally, they conjure up the worst possible scenarios and the most tragic outcomes that trigger debilitating emotional responses. Their mental images and their corresponding feelings become the reason and/or excuses these people use to stay immersed in and engaged with a familiar pain. This group of "sufferers" is far surpassed in number by those who wrestle with, run from, or mentally and emotionally massage their tragic or traumatic past. They are stuck in a story of who they are and what is possible. They have been replaying in their minds a tragic script from which they determine that everything that has happened will more than likely continue to happen. Very often in this scenario, the suffering is evidenced by careless, reckless, self-debasing, or self-injurious behavior. Most often, these are the people who do not believe their lives matter. Very common in both groups is the silent, terrorizing self-talk that keeps them enslaved to circumstances and experiences that destroy their capacity and, often, their desire to lead fulfilling and joyful lives. This level of human suffering is heart wrenching, intense, and absolutely unnecessary.

When I meet individuals who are suffering, whether their experience reflects mental, emotional, or physical pain, I often listen as they try to convince me that they have done everything possible to change their situation. Some people will vehemently challenge and/or reject offers of support and possibilities for remedy. With great precision and detail, they are able to recount the stories of why their efforts didn't work and how they even, in some cases, made the situation worse. I have also met individuals who, because of the depth of the trauma they have lived through, have given up. Resigned to a life of misery, they accept suffering as their fate.

Frequently, my first attempt at offering suffering individuals another way of seeing their experience is met with fierce resistance, which I call "the fight to be right." What I have discovered is that people unwittingly fight to maintain ownership of the very limitations that cause their suffering.

Unfortunately, while fighting for their limitations, most fail to realize this is not a fight they want to win. They are stuck in a way of thinking that triggers certain emotional responses that, in turn, hinder their capacity and diminish their willingness to consider anything new. Rather than engage them in a mental or emotional sparring match, I ask one simple question: "What is your prayer?" When an individual seriously contemplates this question, a tidal wave of reason threatens his or her plausible excuses and reasonable rationales. Stories about how pain and suffering should or can be tolerated and accommodated begin to recede. The ego has very few arguments that can survive the power of an earnest and heartfelt prayer.

No matter how much we would like to blame our suffering on people and circumstances seemingly beyond our control, the bottom line is staggeringly simple: *Anything and everything we experience is a function of what and how we think.* How we think determines our feelings and behavior. How we behave determines the nature and quality of our lives. This also means that any emotional investment (i.e., feelings) that are attached to a particular thought pattern will resurface each time the pattern is engaged or entertained. To neutralize and eventually eliminate an unconscious, unproductive pattern of thought and the associated feelings, a steady stream of new thoughts must be introduced.

I have come to understand that when individuals are suffering through unpleasant or undesirable situations and circumstances, they are often unaware of how they participate in creating or re-creating their experience. In severe cases, when there is an addiction to suffering—meaning that the individuals have accepted their experiences as normal and expect them to remain as they are—there is often a flat-out refusal to acknowledge or accept *We are what we think* as the truth. It is a matter of accepting responsibility for the state and condition of our mind. For some reason, average human beings will resist this premise and the responsibilities associated with it. I, too, have been in that place—resisting, dismissing, and flat-out rejecting the notion that I had the power to change the circumstances of my life with a thought. Regardless of how it was presented to me, I felt as if I was being blamed for my own suffering. It was not until my repeated attempts to "fix" my life had failed that I became ruthlessly committed to having dominion over the circumstances of my life. Only then could I hear, comprehend, and accept how my thoughts, feelings, and patterns of behavior determined my ability to survive, and then thrive. It was not an easy task to undertake or a simple shift to make; however, my desire to be a better example and to create a better life for my children kept me on the path.

In our era of technology-driven lifestyles and social media–based relationships, we have become more attached to our multiple external devices than we are to the power created by our own personal thoughts. The more we are attached to our devices, the more separated we are from our internal, intuitive light. We crave "friends" we have never actually met and virtual "likes" to demonstrate our popularity and acceptance. When our human joys and sorrows are restricted to 140 characters and our most intimate experiences are turned into posts that become cheap fodder for the scrutiny and judgment of online bullies, we are witnessing the ripple effects of our digitized thoughts. If we were to consider how much time we spend seeking external instead of internal validation, the reason why suffering in America—real and imagined—has reached epidemic levels would become clear.

Today, the scales of humanity have tipped perilously toward the lowest common denominator. Due to what has been called the "public prostitution of pain," we have become desensitized to our own suffering because some people are getting paid to put their suffering on display. We have turned human failure, suffering, and dysfunction into the ingredients of highly rated entertainment, dubbing it "reality." While what we watch may in fact be real, there is rarely an antidote offered to address what are, for some, deeply traumatic life experiences. Yet, rather than seeking to eliminate our own suffering or change our own experience, we aim simply to suffer less than others.

Many people have begun to question and challenge these "realities" that are playing out before their eyes and have been inspired to seek a greater sense of dominion in their lives. A growing, inner spiritual imperative demanding that we learn to live more peacefully and authentically has resulted. Men and women of all ages are increasingly ready to accept that there is a spiritual antidote that can transform their traumatic life experiences and the resulting patterns of thoughts, feelings, and behaviors that have produced their suffering. While this approach imposes upon us a great deal of responsibility, it is also a reminder of our inherent and divine power as individuals.

How do we end our suffering? The answer to that question and the premise of *Get Over It!* is not new; in fact, it's very simple. If you do the work to change your thought patterns, your life will change accordingly. In *Get Over It!*, I'm offering you the information, tools, and processes required to make this inner transformation a reality in your life. In other words, I am offering you the work that I call "thought therapy"—a proactive, self-directed, pragmatic daily practice for identifying and transmuting the source of your personal suffering: your dominant negative thought patterns (DNTPs).

Our digital addictions have fostered within us a need for instant information—we want everything fast and easy. The Get Over It! process, which will help to transform the limitations, restrictions, resistance, and possible suffering you may be experiencing in your life, is anything but fast and easy. However, it is *simple*. (There's an important distinction between easy and simple in that it does not take much effort to accomplish this work: a few minutes several times a day is all that's required.) Doing the thought therapy work can be as simple and straightforward as taking your daily vitamins. But only you can purchase your supplements, count out the recommended dosage, pour your beverage, pop the pills in your mouth, and swallow. Consistently making the choice to do something, even something simple, isn't always easy.

The work you are choosing to do to change your thoughts *demands* that you begin to pay attention to what you are thinking, moment by moment. It also requires that you *challenge* long-held thoughts and beliefs by choosing new thoughts that are positive, supportive, and productive. Some would call this "cognitive behavioral therapy." I call it thought therapy, i.e., "getting your mind right so that you can live better." Long before I knew about or studied anything about the so-called therapeutic process commonly used in psychotherapy, I figured out that my mind was a powerful agent for change. It wasn't professional or therapeutic—it was a personal necessity. I had discovered that both conscious and unconscious thoughts are habitual. I realized that every thought we think is attached to a memory, and every memory is attached to a feeling. I came to recognize and believe in my own life that this cycle of thinking and feeling, much of which is unconscious, determined my behavior. After many trials and errors, I understood that if I wanted to change the condition and experience of my life, I had to learn to pay attention to every thought and every feeling so that I could make different choices. To do this, I had to practice and learn to live my "A game," which consists of the 4A's—*awareness, acknowledgment, acceptance,* and *action.* The Get Over It! process will teach you the same.

In much the same way that we receive an alert to notify us when a text message has arrived, we must now create an internal prompt that makes us aware that recurring thoughts have landed and are poised to disrupt our sense of peace and well-being. These are the familiar thoughts, the habitual ones, that we may no longer be aware we are thinking. Don't worry! The Get Over It! process offers you tools that will support you in becoming aware of your thoughts so that you can acknowledge and accept what they are, in order to do something new and facilitate a change in your mind.

Many of the people I have worked with confirm that once they have committed to thought therapy, the work is not hard. Yet the level of commitment necessary often presents great difficulty because the mind is like a muscle: it requires regular workouts to grow stronger. When you stop exercising that muscle, its strength wanes and it grows flabby. Many of us live "flabby" lives because we are unable to make the commitment to consistently do the work necessary to strengthen our minds and thereby improve our lives. We want the full-time rewards for part-time devotion and commitment. But half measures aren't enough! The process I describe in the following pages requires being willing to *do* more, in order to *be* more—and only then will you *have* more. The more committed you are to a life free from mental, emotional, and, in some cases, physical suffering, the more consistent you will be about taking the time required to use the tools presented here. If you commit to doing the work consistently and completely, you'll experience the desired shift within yourself.

Now for the easy part. The primary tools are prayers and affirmations, time-honored spiritual practices that have proven value in the process of changing one's life. These are supported by conscious breath work, thymus thumping, and thought therapy eye movements, which are spiritual energy-clearing tools. When embraced and mastered, these tools can and will alter the biochemistry of your brain.

In this book, you will find 42 prayers and affirmations designed to neutralize and eliminate the most common *dominant negative thought patterns* (DNTPs) that I have encountered throughout my years of working with clients. While most individuals believe that their own childhood traumas, personal situations, and unique life circumstances makes their story and experience different from and worse than everyone else's, I have found this is simply not true.

A playwright friend of mine asserts that there are basically 10 common human dramas. This means that we are all living some version of one of these stories—each set in a unique location, with unique characters, unfolding at a rate of progression unique to us, yet all leading to the same end. But I believe that mental, emotional, and physical suffering are unnecessary and not at all required by the benevolent forces of life. If you currently have the exact opposite of what you desire, I can guarantee that you have an existing dominant negative thought pattern operating in your mind. With consistent prayer and affirmation, your DNTPs can and will be transformed.

Consider this turning point in my history of dominant negative thought patterns:

At one time, I thought and believed that the harder I worked, the more money I would make and the happier I would be. Thoughts are mental energies caused by stimulation to, or activity within, the brain: they are short-lived events that can be generated as an idea or in response to a memory. A feeling is an internal sensation triggered by the central nervous system; they arise as a reaction to, or a response resulting from, either a physical or mental experience or a perception of external stimuli. The DNTP that I held was "You must work hard to make money, and money will make you happy." The thought was "work hard." The feeling was "happy."

In direct competition for space in my mind was another dominant negative thought pattern: "There is never enough." I learned this one during in my childhood and had mastered it for most of my adult life, which gave rise to a great deal of fear and anxiety in my consciousness. What it looked like was this: I would take on more than I could ever expect to accomplish, trying to generate the experience of wealth and happiness I desired, yet believing it would never happen because . . . Not only could I never do enough, there would never be enough time or money or anything else I wanted for me to be truly happy. Sounds crazy, right?

For a good portion of my life, I said yes to everything that was asked of me. I worked long hours, just as I had watched my mom do. I would undertake grueling tasks, just as my grandmother had taught me, in order to prove I could accomplish these tasks even while believing I could not. I made increasing amounts of money that never seemed to fulfill my needs or desires. This interplay of thinking one thing, feeling something else, and doing a third thing—all while believing that you will never get what you want—is what makes suffering seem normal and acceptable to many folks.

The "make more money" part of my pattern was in direct conflict with the "there is never enough" part. The challenge was that I was miserable and tired all the time. I began to resent the people who asked me to do things, and I hated myself for saying yes to them. I also discovered that I was spending more money than I was making because I was too busy to plan expenditures appropriately and wisely. I started praying for an easier life, one in which all my needs were met without so much hard work. It was 1989 when I discovered John Randolph Price's work *The Abundance Book*. He offered a 40-day prayer plan with 10 affirmations that needed to be repeated daily. The plan was to pray consistently—at the same time, in the same place—for 40 days, in order to bring one's mind into alignment with the higher vibration and energy of abundance. He offered one written prayer that had to be signed and dated at the beginning of the process. That, he said, was your contract with the universe and God. Then he gave 10 different affirmations that were to be rotated throughout the process, one a day, to neutralize and override the old thought patterns.

The affirmation that stuck with me and became the new foundation of my life was this: *Money is not my supply. No person, place, or condition is my supply. My awareness, understanding, and knowledge of the all-providing activity of the Divine Mind within me is my supply. My consciousness of this truth is unlimited; therefore, my supply is unlimited.*

That did it for me! I knew that God is the Divine Mind, ever present at all times. Learning to tap into and rely on God, or the Universal Energy of good, opened me to an entirely new way of thinking. Prayer is the way we communicate with God. Affirmation is the way we reprogram the mind. This dynamic thought therapy duo became my ticket out of my DNTPs, my conflicting emotional states of being, and my unproductive ways of behaving. Getting over my habitual thought patterns became a matter of faith, trust, and scientific experimentation.

As a result of the 40-day process, doing what I loved was more beneficial than just working for money. I realized that my life did not have to be hard, and I had no obligation to be miserable to have what I needed and desired. For me, this was more than a shift from negative to positive thinking. My commitment to the thought therapy process of changing my dominant negative thought patterns around money resulted in a major transformation in every area of my life, including my relationships. As a result, I ended a long-term relationship with a married man and published my first book. Over the next few years, I used the process in other areas of my life, including parenting, health issues, and even finding parking spaces. By identifying and neutralizing my own dominant negative thought patterns (i.e., what I had been taught or had come to believe as a result of my experiences), I eliminated the way I voluntarily participated in my own suffering. Lack, limitation, and restriction, whether real or imagined, are all forms of suffering that can be eliminated through awareness, acknowledgment, acceptance, and action.

The Get Over It! process is so much more than a prayer book. It is a remedy for the thoughts and thought patterns that you may not realize you're thinking or holding in consciousness. It is a collaboration between the Divine (God) and your Higher Self that actually becomes your therapist at every stage of the process.

The energy-clearing tools I discuss—conscious breath work, thymus thumping, and thought therapy eye movements— will help build your physical and mental immunity against the impact of the long-held, unconscious, habitual, dominant negative thought patterns that plague your life. They will support the metabolizing or processing of your emotional energy so that you can synthesize and activate the new information you're ingesting through the prayer and affirmation process. They'll also enhance your mental and emotional states of being in a way that will help you integrate and maintain the energetic benefits of this work. In this way, the Get Over It! thought therapy process is a body-mind-spirit experience that will have an impact on all aspects of your being.

The other good thing about the thought therapy process is that it's freely available. Once you've become thoroughly familiar with the process, you'll have a lifelong tool that can and will support you in making immediate and lasting changes in the way your mind operates. The exciting thing I have discovered is that once a dominant negative thought pattern is neutralized, you will be very aware when it attempts to resurface in your mind. On the rare occasions when I find myself thinking a particular thought or feeling a particular way, the affirmative prayer I used to neutralize the thought will immediately pop into my mind. For example, when completing this manuscript, I had a serious encounter with "not good enough." It was rough! Something I read triggered an old feeling, and before I could stop myself, I was knee deep in a tread of self-diminishing thoughts such as these: *The book isn't good enough; I am not a good enough writer; No one will ever buy the book; People are going to criticize me; I am a total and complete failure* . . . Blah, blah, blah. I even wrote my editor and told her so.

As those thoughts began to rampage through my mind, another one surfaced: *Dear God, help me see this rightly.* Instantly, I became aware that I had been working for six hours with no food; it was a beautiful sunny day, and I wanted to go outside; and the chair I was sitting on was starting to hurt my butt. Instead of following the DNTPs to their conclusion, I prayed the prayer for "inadequacy" offered in the book, hit the Save button, and went into my kitchen to make myself a salad. It was just that simple. When I returned to my work 90 minutes later, everything began to flow.

By offering you the Get Over It! process, it is my intention to support you in learning how to:

- Identify negative thoughts (awareness)

- Challenge negative thoughts that cause self-destructive feelings (acknowledgment)

- Replace negative thoughts with more positive ones (acceptance)

- Modify dysfunctional, unproductive, or self-destructive behavior (action)

The way I will coach you through this thought therapy process is by offering you prayers and affirmations written specifically to neutralize your negative thought patterns and the emotional energy most often associated with those patterns. As a spiritual technician, I am offering you psycho-spiritual tools instead of traditional psychological ones. And if you are participating in traditional psychotherapy or counseling, all the better. This process is totally compatible with and supportive of traditional therapies. What I know to be true is that most of you will never end up on a therapist's couch. This does not mean that you cannot get help or be helped. The Get Over It! process is a deeply spiritual thought therapy that will deprogram and reprogram your mind, shifting your habitual thoughts and feelings in a way that supports your desire to "get over" anything and everything that may be holding you back.

Even if you cannot identify your *exact* DNTP, working with the prayer, affirmation, and one or more of the energy-clearing tools of a DNTP that is closely related to what you are experiencing will have a powerful impact. Neutralizing any one negative thought pattern will bring you face-to-face with the one that has been most difficult for you to identify. The goal here is to modify how you think and change the emotional energy attached to the unconscious and habitual patterns of thinking. If you engage in the Get Over It! process under the watchful eye of your Higher Self, and you set a clear intention, you will receive exactly what you need. The most important element of this process is willingness— willingness to know, willingness to change, and willingness to heal and grow. Along with willingness, you must be ready.

The real test will come when you become aware that what and how you have been thinking have created some of your most difficult challenges. At that point, your ego will rise to slam you up against a wall of disbelief and resistance. You will come face-to-face with the intimate details of your most debilitating and self-defeating stories. You will be tempted to curse me and put this book on a shelf with all the other self-help books that you didn't complete. Now that you are forewarned, here is your prescription: *Don't do that—pray!* I am offering you a Universal Clearing Prayer in Chapter 5 that you can apply to any situation. If that doesn't work, turn to any page in Chapter 7 and pray any prayer. Once you come back into your "right mind," continue to do the work.

The light of your soul is your bridge to a better experience of yourself and your life. Just as some electrical current flows through the walls of your home, some energetic current flows through your body. In the same way that you can flip a switch to tap into your home's electrical current and turn on the lights in a room, you can tap into the currents of energy that run through you and brighten the light in your soul. Flipping the switch to turn off your DNTPs will accomplish that. The work I'm offering you here is designed to rewire your thinking to make better use of your connection to Divine Mind so your soul light can shine.

If you are ready, willing, and committed, there's never been a better time or a greater need for you to share your infinite light. Remember these words as you begin this process: simple and easy; ready and willing; awareness, acknowledgment, acceptance, and action. Ready? Set? Let's do this work!

PART I
THE FIGHT TO BE RIGHT

◆

CHAPTER 1

MS. CLAUDIE'S FILES

We cannot change anything
if we cannot change our thinking.

—SANTOSH KALWAR

*P*eople do what they do in response to what they think (i.e., the information that they have and how they interpret it) in the moment of a particular experience. Often, what people do makes absolutely no sense to those who are watching them, and even less sense to the ones who are engaged in blind, irresponsible, or self-destructive behavior. It's not easy to watch loved ones go through a difficult experience. It's even more difficult when the someone who is going through the difficult experience is you!

When friends or loved ones who patiently listen to your too-often-repeated tale of woe speak those three simple words—

"Get over it!"—you may feel exasperated. Sometimes, it's the tone of their voice. Oftentimes, it's just not what you need or want to hear. In all situations, under all circumstances, the message behind those three words is so much easier said than done. Those words—"Get over it!"—dismiss your difficult situation and your accompanying negative feelings as irrelevant, unimportant, or unacceptable, even though to you they are just the opposite. In many instances, by the time you hear those words come at you or reverberate through you, you've been stuck in a mental, emotional, or spiritual dead end for some time.

Life is hard! Just ask newly single moms with no child support, displaced autoworkers in cities stripped of manufacturing, downsized fifty-somethings with no retirement savings, or stigmatized men and women returning to society after years of incarceration. It's *hard* to reestablish yourself after a divorce. It's *hard* to cover your basic expenses and stay on top of your student loans. It's hard to face a family health crisis when you have little or no insurance coverage. Even people who have done their best to do the right things, in the right way, at the right time may still find themselves facing astonishingly hard times and challenging situations.

Yet those who know the true meaning of achievement will tell you that their accomplishments were never entirely due to what they did or what happened for them. Something also had to exist *within* them. We're all overly familiar with the painful tales of a person who found personal, professional, or financial success then lost it because of poor choices or bad behavior. Whether you're working toward it or had it and lost it, the level of fulfillment anyone finds and enjoys in this lifetime all boils down to this: how you think determines what you experience.

The thoughts we have, the beliefs we hold, and the behaviors we engage in when we are going through a life challenge or upset often leave a deep imprint on our consciousness. It's the little things that determine the quality of our lives. Little slights, little disappointments, little upsets piled one on top of another can become a mental or emotional catastrophe if they are not addressed. When these "little things" are added to the myriad of random childhood traumas and critical life changes we've all experienced, it's no wonder many of us have no clue how to deal with what we think or feel at any given moment.

When we consider the debilitating human conditions so many people have lived through and lived with, "Get over it" seems tantamount to saying, "Stop whining and complaining." That would probably work well if we could simply wash our brains out as a way to facilitate our forgetting. When we have been through something that has left a negative imprint on us, more than just our brains have been affected. What about our hearts? What about our spirits? These aspects of who we are that are also involved in the process of getting over something cannot be washed clean so easily. And these are the aspects of ourselves that bear the brunt of our difficult life experiences. Considering the power of the mind to create, the capacity of the heart to ache, and the energy carried in the spirit, getting over life's most difficult experiences can take more than just a positive mind-set, the insistence of a friend, and a good mental shampoo.

DOMINANT THOUGHT PATTERNS

One of life's simplest yet most powerful truths is this: What we consistently think about and how we think about it will eventually show up in reality. Mahatma Gandhi, a man who accomplished the impossible, said that men often become what they believe. "If I believe I cannot do something, it makes me incapable of doing it. But when I believe I can, then I acquire the ability to do it even if I didn't have it in the beginning." Understanding what we consistently think about and how we feel in the midst of those thoughts is not an esoteric or New Age concept. It is a scientific fact, one formulated from actual data that has determined a direct link exists between our dominant thoughts, our emotions, and our actions.

Research indicates that the average person has between 60,000 and 80,000 thoughts a day, of which 60 to 75 percent are unconscious, meaning you are not aware that you are thinking these thoughts. Mental health professionals and scientists alike have concluded that the goal cannot be to control every thought. That would be a futile exercise in today's world of overstimulation and the proliferation of digital devices. Instead, it is our dominant negative thoughts and beliefs that can and must be the focus of attention.

A dominant thought is an automatic repetitive idea that creates a deep tread, or impression, in the brain. It is a thought or pattern of thoughts attached to a specific and frequently repeated emotional response. Our lives are shaped by our most dominant thoughts because these are the thoughts that mold our beliefs. Beliefs direct our expectations and actions. Actions determine the results we get in our lives.

THE SUBCONSCIOUS MIND

Dominant thoughts or beliefs determine how we live our lives because they are stored in the subconscious mind, the aspect of the mind that works nonstop to create whatever we think about. When the mind is consciously or unconsciously focused on traumatic experiences, unpleasant memories, and a long list of the things you "do not" want to experience, the energy of these thoughts becomes dominant in your mind and takes over as the basis of the mental attitude that governs your expectations. In life, you do not experience what you ask for; you experience what you expect. The expectations we hold are the fruits of the subconscious mind.

The subconscious mind is your memory bank, the cloud storage for all your life's data. All your experiences, cultural nuances, learned knowledge, positive or negative memories, and achievements and failures are stored in the subconscious mind. It is the aspect of the mind that never sleeps. These subconscious thoughts become stimulated when you're faced with a choice or a decision, or when you're weighing pros and cons, possibilities and consequences. Any choice about what you do next will stimulate a memory about what has happened before. The subconscious mind will sort through your memory bank for anything similar or familiar to what you're facing in the moment, and you won't be aware that your mind is doing it. The implications of this unconscious mental sorting process explain why we all act and react the way we do.

THE HUMAN COMPUTER BRAIN

Most thought is generated or directed by one of three primary conscious goals: understanding information, manipulating information, or generating and creating information. When an experience requires an *understanding* of information, the brain will recall, summarize, categorize, and assign a role to the information received. This is a psychological and evaluative process. Since the goal is understanding, evaluation of each thought, idea, or impulse related to the goal is considered. In the process of *manipulating* information, the brain will analyze, apply, induce, deduce, and problem solve. Manipulation requires the application of established beliefs and rules to produce a result or decision. This is a comparative process of thought, one in which, like a computer, the brain pieces together preexisting patterns to create new thought pathways without a qualitative assessment of the information being considered. In this way, the process of manipulating information is limited and uncreative. When *generating* or *creating* information, the brain will synthesize, predict, evaluate, and question. This is a process of the intellect working in harmony with emotion. Thought is generated in response to the impulses experienced within the body. Unfortunately, when intellectual awareness ends or negative energy is encountered, cooperation between thought and feeling ends. Thought then becomes focused on understanding or manipulating the information, which can be either a positive or negative process.

The human brain is believed to be a much better computer than any man-made computer ever created because it is capable of processing information in two separate areas: the conscious mind and the subconscious mind. Understanding, manipulating, and generating or creating information takes place in the realm of the conscious mind. Deciding what to eat for dinner, formulating a response to a coworker you don't like, figuring out how to resolve the shortage in the monthly budget, and remembering how cute your six-month-old son is are all conscious activities that move through the brain simultaneously.

According to the Laboratory of Neuro Imaging at the University of Southern California, the average person has about 48.6 conscious thoughts per minute. That equals about 70,000 thoughts per day. Other experts estimate that the mind thinks between 60,000 to 80,000 conscious and subconscious thoughts a day, averaging 2,500 to 3,300 thoughts per hour, which is incredible. However, if we could pay attention to each thought, we would discover that most of them are useless, unimportant bits of information that pass through the mind at warp speed. The random words we repeat, the observations the mind makes that we never speak aloud, repetitive thoughts about something we heard, songs we remember from long ago, questions about nothing meaningful, answers to questions we no longer remember, and a lot of stray facts pop in and out of the mind every moment. And it is these thoughts that create the long-standing patterns of thought and the beliefs that create major blockages and obstacles in our lives. These are the thoughts that originate in the subconscious mind.

Once the conscious mind processes, sorts, and makes sense of the data received, it passes on the information to the subconscious mind. The subconscious mind is the supercomputer. It is believed to be 80 times more powerful than the conscious mind because it finds patterns and relations faster, can deal with much more complex data, and even simulates things much better than your conscious mind. Unlike the conscious mind, which executes the desired function and then moves on to something new, the subconscious mind continues to process data from the moment it receives the information to the moment it finds an answer. Millions of thoughts are processed each day. Researchers have determined that the subconscious thought process remains active while you are asleep. The subconscious mind compares and analyzes all incoming data with everything that is in your memory—anything you may have ever seen, heard, known, or understood—until it finds a pattern or solution. And it is the subconscious patterning process that determines your state of mind or consciousness.

Just in case this sounds or feels too scientific for you, let me break it down. We have thousands of thoughts that we don't know we're thinking. These thoughts have memories and feelings attached to them. When we encounter a familiar or similar experience that generates a familiar or similar feeling, the brain generates a familiar or similar thought. Sometimes we're aware of the thought associated with the feeling, but most often we're not aware of the thought. The thoughts that we don't know we're thinking generate feelings that are so familiar, we assume that what we're going through in the moment is the same as something we've been through before. This motivates us to do or not do specific things in order to avoid unwanted or unpleasant outcomes. This is what it means to be stuck.

31

Because there are millions of thoughts being processed through your mind every minute, there is no way for you to be aware of them all. The conscious mind that evaluates and records thoughts has no access to them until the subconscious mind pushes the results of its processing into the conscious mind. If we add to this equation the external stimuli received from the physical world that gives rise to sensory sensations and new thoughts, it's easy to see why it has been so difficult to determine what comes first, the thought or the feeling.

NEGATIVE VERSUS POSITIVE EXPERIENCES

Everyone, at one time or another, entertains negative thoughts. The challenge comes when we pay homage to them by entertaining them repeatedly. It is then that negative thoughts become habitual, unconscious, and pattern forming. For example have you ever said, "Don't come too close to me, you might catch my cold"? Of course you have. Conversely, have you ever said, "Don't come too close to me, you might catch my beauty or my brilliance"? Probably not. Because of our dominant negative thoughts, we often go through life repeating the same mistakes over and over again, experiencing the very things we *do not* want because the programming imprinted in our minds has us, essentially, riding a merry-go-round. It takes more energy to process a negative experience than it does to process a positive experience. When something unpleasant occurs, the mind will linger on the thought and experience to figure it out. "Why did that happen to me?" "Why did she say that to me?" "Why did he do that to me?" The more unpleasant, difficult, challenging, or frightening the experience was, the more thoughts the mind will process in connection to it.

As human beings, we hate to be wrong, we want to avoid being hurt, and we always want to be seen in a positive light. When negative feedback, destructive criticism, or unwanted correction comes at us, it not only triggers an attachment to similar past events, it deflates our good intentions in the present moment. When we add mental and emotional triggers (e.g., the environment, authority figures, or emotional connections we have to certain people or things) to the circumstances of our current experience, the resulting negative or traumatic outcome only deepens the subconscious imprint that may already exist in the brain.

This is not the same process the mind engages in for a positive experience. Rarely do we ask ourselves, "Why is this good thing happening to me?" or "How can I create more of the pleasant feeling?" In fact, more often than not, when something really wonderful or pleasant comes our way, we might even say, "I can't believe this is happening to me." When we have a good or pleasant experience, we may remember it and even talk about it, but we do not mull it over. We take it in and move on. A pleasant experience may leave us feeling good or uplifted, but as soon as we hit a bump in the road, we forget the good and focus once more on the not so good. This happens because the negative, traumatic, unhealed mental and emotional imprints from childhood experiences are activated each time you face a similar, or what feels like a familiar, situation.

CORE BELIEFS

We all have a file of beliefs about ourselves and our lives based on stories we've heard or stories we've made up in reaction to experiences we've had. Some of those beliefs are positive; some of them are negative. The negative beliefs are the ones that create many of the challenges and issues we face in every aspect of life. We focus repeatedly on the negative stories and, more often than not, we are unconsciously fueled by negative emotional energy. These patterns of thought or core beliefs not only define our behaviors, assumptions, and expectations, they become the foundation for our understanding of how the world works and what we can/will/do expect from others.

As a psychological construct, a core belief is the essence of how we see, evaluate, and assess ourselves, other people, and the world. Core beliefs are often formed based on interpretations we made in childhood of what we saw, heard, or were led to believe was true about who we are. The way our adult caregivers responded to our behavior when we were children had a tremendous influence on the formation of our core beliefs. These subconscious core beliefs are triggered, once we reach adulthood, by situations that are similar to and closely aligned with experiences we had as children.

Sharon, an ambitious paralegal who often engaged in critical thinking or problem solving, was completely unaware of the power of her core beliefs. However, she did notice that she had difficulty when it came to standing up for herself and sharing her perspective in situations involving both her work colleagues and her family members. Sharon recognized that in those situations, she often second-guessed herself. Even when she felt strongly about something, she would surrender her ideas, needs, or wants to the loudest or strongest personality in the room. The problem was intensified with the men she dated, whom she felt often dismissed or ignored her requests or desires.

After several months of therapy and work with a coach, Sharon became aware that in the presence of a strong personality, she felt that what she had to say was not important. She recognized that this was the same pattern she'd experienced growing up with her brother, a star football player, who'd always gotten the lion's share of her parents' time, attention, and praise. In fact, Sharon remembered that whenever she tried to talk to her father about something she needed or wanted, he would tell her, "That's not important right now. I've got to help your brother with something." Her mother would often say, "I know you think it's important, but it can wait."

Sharon often felt that her desires were subjugated to whatever her brother needed or wanted and therefore she was not important. As a result, while Sharon was always able to do for others and meet their needs, she had a difficult time asking for what she wanted or needed. After working with her therapist and coach, Sharon identified the core belief that who she was, what she wanted, and what she had to say were "not important."

Core beliefs, such as Sharon's, develop over time. They are strongly held and often inflexible because they are maintained by the tendency to focus on information that supports the belief while ignoring the information and experiences that contradict it. Although Sharon was often praised for her excellent work and told how valuable she was to the team of attorneys she was associated with, she could not hold on to those positive experiences in situations that reminded her of her childhood. For Sharon, even neutral situations or statements were interpreted as negatives, reinforcing her "unimportance" once again.

After years of holding the dominant negative thought "I'm not important," and of feeling the anger and sadness that accompanied that thought, Sharon's core belief had become so strong that she no longer questioned it. She accepted it and vigilantly looked for and listened for evidence to support what she had been taught to believe. Since we always get what we expect, Sharon found more than enough evidence in her daily life to motivate self-sabotaging behaviors like remaining silent, acting invisible, and isolating.

Dominant negative thought patterns are often so ingrained in consciousness that people are often totally unaware that these patterns have become a core belief, a permanent filter through which the individuals see themselves and the world. In fact, many people argue against their own dominant negative thought patterns and core beliefs by mentally jumping to the opposite end of the continuum just to prove that they don't believe what they actually do believe. In this way, they create a polarized thought pattern to contradict the discomfort of their core beliefs.

For example, Andy, like Sharon, held an unconscious core belief that he was not important. He contradicted and camouflaged his supposed inadequacy by acting out with a sense of entitlement and arrogance. Andy decided that his needs, wants, opinions, and desires were superior to those of others and had to be accommodated at all costs. This inflated behavior, motivated by the need to prove his importance, began to strike others as aggressive. In fact, over time, Andy was regarded as a bully. Attempts to cover up unconscious core beliefs and the dominant negative thought patterns that create them can result in extremely polarized beliefs and behaviors.

THOUGHTS AND CONSEQUENCES

Something happens, which triggers you to have a thought. The thought you have generates a feeling, a sensation that moves throughout your body. Depending upon the energy of the feeling, you behave in a particular way. In the midst of this reaction, you have a series of other thoughts—some of which you are aware of, others of which you are not. Each of your conscious and unconscious thoughts also has a feeling attached to it, a feeling that either motivates or restricts your behavior. Alternatively, you may have a feeling, a sensation that moves throughout your body, that gives rise to a thought. That thought then motivates you to behave in a particular way— to do or not do something—which prompts a series of other thoughts . . . and the cycle continues. Regardless of which comes first, the thought or the feeling, this vastly simplified version of how the mind works happens thousands of times per minute, whether or not you are aware that it is going on.

Everything we think, say, or do is attached to something we have heard, seen, or done. That's just the way it works. The brain stores information: the scent of your grandmother's house, your child's first cry, the exact shade of blue of a certain dress, the flavor of a ripe tomato. Our memories compose those experiences that have already unfolded in our lives. Memories give us a sense of who and what we are in the world. The mind works to tie our past to our present in order to provide a framework for how we interpret the future. It is this process of storing and referencing a collective set of memories that makes us who we are. This all works fine and dandy when the stored memories are powerful, productive, and familiar. The challenge comes when our past was disjointed, dysfunctional, or traumatic. Things can be even more difficult when we face the uncertainty of the unknown.

When something unknown or unfamiliar comes to us, how we receive it, respond to it, or react because of it is determined by what is already present in our consciousness. Scientists guestimate that 99 percent of what we perceive about the world around us is a function of what is already present in our minds. This is supported and explained by *A Course in Miracles,* Lesson #2, which states, "I have given everything I see all the meaning that it has for me." The meanings we give to people, situations, circumstances, and experiences is almost always directed and dictated by our dominant thought patterns, whether positive or negative. For the purposes of the Get Over It! process, we will focus on negative thought patterns; those are the ones that make it hard for us to move beyond the places that we are familiar with or stuck in.

MEET MS. CLAUDACIOUS PUTTITIN

Allow me to introduce you to Ms. Claudie Puttitin. She lives in your brain; in fact, she lives in the brain of every single human being on the planet. Ms. Claudie, a 65-year-old spinster librarian, works 24 hours a day. She's never been in love, never had a lover. Needless to say, she's wound a bit tight. She doesn't get out much because she's totally committed to her work. Allow her image to fill your mind right now. She's about 5 feet 2 inches and slim in stature. She hasn't been shopping in quite a while and has never wasted a dime on a fashion magazine. Every single day of her life she wears a plaid skirt, a pinstriped blouse, and a cardigan sweater with the top button buttoned. She wears support stockings and lace-up orthopedic shoes—you know, the kind with the puffy round toes. Her 27-inch-long salt-and-pepper hair is arranged neatly in a bun at the back of her head. This is where she sticks her pencils, paper clips, and an occasional pack of gum to keep her going throughout the day. Of course, she wears glasses! And when she's not wearing them, they hang from a black cord around her neck. She swears by the Playtex Cross Your Heart bra because it makes her very small breasts appear to be very pointy. Can you see her? Do you feel her presence?

Ms. Claudie's job is to file every thought, feeling, belief, word, and experience that you've ever had into the filing cabinet of your mind. She does this second by second, minute by minute, every day of your life. Her work began the moment you were first able to feel and respond to a sensation, even when you didn't possess language to describe your experiences. In other words, her work began when you were in the womb.

The first files that Ms. Claudie created for you were in response to what your mother was thinking or feeling, which in turn created a sensation in your body. This is an important reference point because some of the sensations you respond to in your present life may very well have nothing to do with you. You may still be reacting to thoughts or feelings your mother had that you picked up as sensations prior to your birth.

Your every "womb time" wriggle or twitch, whether pleasant or not, was labeled and filed away by Ms. Claudie. At first, she used simple words based on her long-term knowledge and connection to the human experience. Words like "happy" or "sad" and "good" or "bad" were the only categories she needed when you were an infant. The moment you developed language skills and began to associate words to thoughts and feelings, however, her work became much more complex. Anything and everything you experienced had to be classified by feelings and thoughts, then placed in a file labeled with the associated dominant energy. When you were hungry, when you fell off the bed, when you heard somebody screaming—not at you but around you—Ms. Claudie selected an existing file or, when necessary, created a new file, then tucked that thought or feeling inside. On those occasions when you were young and very active—a time when you kept her extremely busy—she may have misfiled certain things, placing some thoughts or feelings in an already existing file, one for familiar- or similar-feeling experiences.

The "good thoughts" files became the home for thoughts you had following good, very good, and awesome experiences, because your body generated similar-feeling reactions or energies in response to them. The "unhappy thoughts" files became the home for thoughts you had following sad, lonely, and unhappy experiences, because your body generated similar-feeling reactions and energies to these experiences. She created files for other thoughts and feelings as well—those prompted by anger, fear, jealousy, regret, and so forth. The older you got, and the more sophisticated your thought processes became, the more dominant energy categories Ms. Claudie had to sort through to find the file she needed.

Around the time you turned six years old, Ms. Claudie had to streamline her process to keep up with the work of maintaining the filing system within your mind. She began to rely totally on the sensations associated with your experiences to determine into which file your thoughts and feelings should be placed. It may have become a little sloppy, but Ms. Claudie is, after all, up there in age, and needing to classify and file roughly 70,000 thoughts per day created a great deal of running back and forth between file cabinets.

Needless to say, some files are much larger than others, and some files you'd expect to find don't even exist. It doesn't matter whether you've had a specific experience one time or ten times, when Ms. Claudie opens a file, all of your past thoughts and feelings associated with that dominant energy come rushing to the surface. We call the outcome of this mental process "remembering." Now, here's the kicker: some things that get filed away aren't even yours! Things you hear, see, or feel—whether or not they have anything to do with you—end up in some file in your brain. Unfortunately, while Ms. Claudie may be very good at putting stuff in files, she isn't always particularly accurate.

I'm not blaming Ms. Claudie for the unpleasant, negative, or traumatic memories that get stored in our brains. She is simply doing her divinely assigned work. The brain sorts and categorizes and stores everything—that is simply how the brain functions. The challenge we all face includes shifting how we interpret our experiences so that the energies we hold on to, which are associated with those experiences, do not further expand our already-bulging dominant negative thought files.

Thoughts and images control the mind. Whether pleasant or unpleasant, conscious or unconscious, our dominant thoughts deepen the imprints of specific thought patterns and expand their related files. Ms. Claudie's file categories and our propensity to get stuck in the negative explain why our minds will focus on negative experiences so much more than on the positive ones—the files containing negative thoughts, feelings and experiences are simply much larger than those containing positive thoughts, feelings and experiences. Reducing our dominant negative thought files requires consistently acting, thinking, and speaking in a positive fashion. *What you focus on grows!*

According to Dr. Ellen Weber of the MITA International Brain Center, "The brain is equipped to change rapidly and biologically reshape itself." The process, called "neuroplasticity," one of the most popular areas of research in psychology today, refers to the brain's ability to restructure itself after training or practice. This scientific research is great news. It can also be the primary motivation for you to make the commitment to engage the Get Over It! thought therapy process. Your brain can be reprogrammed. *Hallelujah!* So, no matter how dysfunctional you may think you are, no matter how much trauma you may have endured, there is a way out—if you are willing to do the work.

Neuroplasticity is what makes personal growth and mental development possible at the most basic level. With the understanding that change is indeed possible, we are now able to focus on the ways in which you'd like to grow.

Ms. Claudie has done all of the foundational work on your behalf. She created the files, the memories, that have made you who you are today. However, Ms. Claudie's files are not all of who you are, nor is it who and what you must remain.

When it comes to who you believe you are and who you might become, Ms. Claudie doesn't have a file for that yet, because you have not yet provided this new information. Today is the day to begin doing the work required to attach new sensations to old words, to give new definitions to old sensations. Ms. Claudie will be happy to create the necessary new files.

CHAPTER 2

THE 4A'S: AWARENESS, ACKNOWLEDGMENT, ACCEPTANCE, AND ACTION

The ancestor of every action is a thought.

—RALPH WALDO EMERSON

*I*f you ever want to become aware—perhaps painfully aware—of what you are thinking and the patterns present in your mind, look at your life. Look at the condition of your home environment, the people with whom you have fulfilling (or not-so-fulfilling) relationships, the experiences you seem destined to repeat over and over, the job you go to day in and day out, the status of your bank account. Now consider what you believe is missing in your life . . . Everything you are experiencing is a function of your files, or what you are thinking.

Another way to increase your awareness of your dominant negative thought patterns is to closely examine what you think about other people. Here is a series of truths that is often difficult for people to recognize or accept: if you can see it out there, it exists—or has at some point existed— within you. Some of what you see, you have been or don't want to be. Most of what you see, you believe you are. All of what you see—out there in the world or attached to other people—is a thought that is already present in your mind.

"I give meaning to everything I see" is a lesson from *A Course in Miracles.* It can be translated to mean the following: "I see it because I recognize it. I recognize it because I believe I am it. Because I believe I am it, the ego demands that I hide it and make it all about you." Making your life conditions and experiences about something or someone other than yourself "trumps" the truth that thoughts, not people, create the intimate and personal conditions of your life.

Once upon a time, when I was an average human being who had done no personal development or emotional healing work, I was clueless about my dominant negative thoughts. I suffered from what I call "trumpitis" thoughts that reoccurred at a rapid pace, motivating certain impulsive behaviors. Remember, every thought has a feeling or memory attached to it. Whether a thought triggers a feeling or a feeling generates a thought really doesn't matter. What matters is becoming aware of how the energy of a thought/feeling combo motivates behavior and generates certain expectations. What matters is knowing that there are mental files governing your life. What matters is learning how to use four powerful spiritual principles to support you in identifying, and hopefully eliminating, your dominant negative thought patterns.

PUTTING THE 4A'S INTO PRACTICE

Awareness, acknowledgment, acceptance, and action—the 4A's—are the four spiritual building blocks that, when used appropriately, can help move us through the upsets, challenges, and detours created by how and what we think. They can help counterbalance and neutralize the unconscious, habitual demands of the ego that feed on dominant negative thought patterns and open our minds to new ways of thinking and being. The 4A's capture the essence of a simple prayer I have learned to say when my mind is running amuck: *Dear Lord, help me see this rightly. Let there be light!*

The 4A's are designed to alert you to the hidden dominant negative thought patterns that are influencing the tides of your life experience. This does not mean you have done or are doing anything wrong. This is simply an effort to support you in becoming conscious of what you are thinking so that you can choose to change your mind.

AWARENESS

Awareness, like everything else, is subject to the laws of natural order; in other words, you must be aware something exists before you can choose to do something about it. The natural order of life never takes us into experiences we are not equipped to handle; those are experiences to which we contribute, with no awareness of our doing so. As we become aware of our defenses, excuses, rationales, limiting beliefs, and misinterpretations of reality, we are equipped to make better choices. Awareness of our strengths can minimize the impact of our weaknesses. In all life experiences, awareness that what you are doing is not bringing forth the desired result serves as a "divine intervention" in support of healing and growth. Even when the issue, pattern, or wound to be healed is unpleasant or painful, awareness is a precursor to acknowledgment. The flip side of awareness is denial (a resistance to knowing or becoming aware).

As a principle of healing, awareness also opens the energy of the heart. It makes us more compassionate because it reminds us of our human weaknesses and frailties. Once the heart is opened, the natural flow of life transforms awareness into the knowledge and understanding required to move beyond the places in which we are stuck, the patterns of thought, belief, and behavior that create and re-create painful experiences. In the healing process, awareness makes us more compassionate toward ourselves and others because it provides the information we need to make self-supportive and conscious choices.

ACKNOWLEDGMENT

Acknowledgment is the first step toward healing because it moves awareness to a higher level. Once you become aware that something exists, you are required to acknowledge your awareness. Acknowledgment is, therefore, the conscious and/or verbal recognition of what you know and understand now. It is an act of courageous ownership that requires a willingness to tell the radical truth about what is going on and your role in the unfolding events. To acknowledge means that you recognize a thing for what it is; you own it as a conscious or unconscious creation. Until and unless we acknowledge something, we cannot and will not be able to unravel or heal the details of the experience.

Acknowledgment takes us beyond the dramatic details of our story and down into the nitty-gritty of our role in whatever is being revealed to us about ourselves. As an empowering healing principle, acknowledgment is about leveraging our awareness and owning what we have or have not done, even when we may not understand what motivated that behavior or choice. Our behaviors and choices are our contributions to our experiences. Regardless of what we may say we need, want, or desire at any given moment, what shows up in our lives as our experience is what we think and feel about those things. Until we become aware of and acknowledge our contributions, we will blame, feel victimized, and cling to powerlessness. Acknowledgment is a declaration of our unconscious dominant negative thought patterns that are hidden beneath the surface and must ultimately be accepted to be healed.

ACCEPTANCE

While we may not like what is going on—while it may be difficult, uncomfortable, or downright painful—there comes a point when we must simply admit that what shows up in our lives is a function of our thoughts. The most common alternatives to acceptance are fear, resistance, denial, and against-ness. Each of these serves to make a difficult experience more difficult. Fear will motivate you to lie about what you know. Resistance will motivate you to justify what you think and feel. Denial will lead you away from ownership into victimization. And against-ness will motivate you to fight to be right when you are absolutely dead wrong. Acceptance means resolve, not resignation. Resolve leads to victory, while resignation makes us victims. Resolve is the higher vibratory position of "This is what it is. I am going to learn from it and move through it with dignity and ease." When we're resigned, we adopt the position of powerlessness or helplessness, meaning, "Oh well, this happened to me and there's nothing else I can do."

Acceptance does not mean agreement, nor does it mean we feel good about what we're facing. It does, however, mean that we're willing to look for and embrace the lesson. It also indicates a willingness to grow through the experience by understanding something "bigger," which we may not recognize just yet, is unfolding for our benefit.

ACTION

Remember, no matter what shows up, there is always something we can do, some action we can take, to advance our healing, growth, and learning. In most cases, awareness, acknowledgment, and acceptance will take the sting out of an experience and get you to where you need to be. In other cases, you will be required to do (or not do) something to evolve and come out on the other end of an experience unscathed. If you can acknowledge your role in the experience and accept that you are healing and learning the truth about your own dominant thought patterns, you will be guided to act and take your next most appropriate steps.

Learning and using the 4A's is one of the most effective methods for tuning into and eliminating your DNTPs. You do this by learning to pay attention to what you are thinking and the feelings being generated by your thoughts. Once you become aware that a DNTP has been triggered through evidence or experience, *acknowledge* it to yourself.

Then accept whatever thought/behavior pattern is operating and prepare to act. In this way, the Get Over It! process will work for you and through you, almost like magic.

THE UNHAPPY HOURS

Consider the tale of Christie and Bruce. Because Christie had no knowledge of the 4A's, Ms. Claudie had to spend countless overtime hours sorting and filing the mountain of disowned DNTPs generated during the "Unhappy Hours."

Christie met Bruce at her favorite bar's happy hour. Not only was he good looking, he was the first guy she had met in a long time who seemed to want more than sex. After they exchanged numbers, he called when he said he would, and their conversations were quite stimulating and fun. Christie refused to allow herself to get too excited too quickly because she knew that happy-hour guys just cannot be trusted. Bruce was a new experience for Christie. She had no mental file in which to place the experience she was having, so, instead, her experience triggered old thoughts and feelings. She thought about the other guys she had met in bars. She thought about how foul and nasty those experiences had been. She thought about how she kept hoping against hope that each one would be *the* one, only to be disappointed when she got exactly what she had gotten previously. Triggered by her memories, these thoughts were so strong that they blinded her to her current reality and the possibility that Bruce could actually be a really nice guy. Each thought trigger that came into Christie's mind also had a feeling attached to it. For Christie, those feelings included fear of being wrong again; disappointment with herself for not being able to "attract" the right guy; and cynicism, which for her sounded like, "Here comes another one, just like the other one."

Like most of us, Christie was totally unaware that she had been triggered and was, therefore, digging through the old files that held all of her beliefs about herself in relationship to men. After all, she had file cabinets full of the evidence. She had been there, done that—and had it done to her more times than she cared to remember. Unfortunately, she did remember, and that was the problem. It is clear that Christie's DNTP about never finding the right man had been triggered, so rather than paying close attention to how Bruce was being with her, she was engaged in her thoughts about him. Thought triggers, those things you are inclined to believe will always be true, can serve as your DNTP "smoke detectors." They warn that a particular thought is about to catch fire. If you let the fire start due to lack of awareness, you risk having your house burn down. Christie was totally unaware of the five-alarm fire raging in her mind, so she kept dating Bruce because she just refused to be wrong—again. Remember, thinking one thing, feeling something else, and behaving in a manner that is incongruent with what you think and what you feel is the stuff that makes suffering normal.

They had been on three dates before Bruce asked if he could kiss her good night. After that first kiss, Bruce told her that he liked her a lot and hoped that they could build something solid between them. Christie was floored (i.e., excited, because things seemed promising) and at the same time suspicious (i.e., mistrustful, because thought triggers that contradicted what she was feeling had been activated). Her DNTP was about to singe the memories scattered around her mind. She told him that she hoped that they could, too, but that she also lived by the 90-day rule: no sex for the first 90 days in a new relationship. He agreed that would be a great way for them really to get to know each other, and he was ready to give it a try.

The next three months flew by with standing Tuesday- and Thursday-night dates, lots of laughter, and many deep conversations. Bruce appeared to be a nice guy, and he seemed to be into her, but Christie was still leery about his true intentions. She had been down this road before: Larry, she had discovered after a year of dating, had been married; Douglas had had two other women on the side; and her ex-husband had a secret gambling problem that left her bankrupt and heartbroken. How had she managed to find such a nice guy after a series of losers? Christie and Bruce dated for almost seven months before they were intimate. Despite her ongoing reservations, by the third time Bruce spent the night, Christie had met his family and knew about all his exes. Yet she was still determined to discover what he was really up to. Christie was "nobody's fool," she boasted to her friends, and she was determined to protect herself from any more unhappy endings.

One night while Bruce was sleeping, Christie decided to do a pocket search and a phone check. His pockets were empty, and his telephone was password protected, but in his wallet she found a credit card with a woman's name on it. *Bull's-eye!* This was all Christie needed to justify her suspicions. On their next date, when Bruce reached for his wallet to pay the check, Christie snatched it out of his hands and rummaged through it, looking for the credit card. Unable to find it, she asked him in a not-so-polite voice, "Why don't you pay for it with her card?"

"What the f*** are you talking about?" Bruce said, stunned and embarrassed.

Oh! So, he curses, too! Christie thought to herself. *That's new.* "You know *exactly* what I'm talking about. I saw a card in your wallet with a woman's name on it. Who is she? Where is *that* card?"

"You searched my wallet?" After the initial shock, Bruce was more sad than angry.

"You're damned right I did! I tried to get into your telephone, too, but it was locked."

"Come on, Christie," he hissed. "Let me take you home."

"F*** you! I'll take Uber." Christie stood up and walked away, then disappeared into the ladies' room. Bruce, still at the table, gaped after her.

Fifteen minutes later, when she darted for the door, Bruce stepped in front of her and said, "I'm not that guy, Christie. I brought you here, and I will take you home."

His voice was so calm, gentle, yet commanding that Christie felt obligated to follow him to the car.

They rode to her front door in silence. After he stopped the car and turned the motor off, he reached for her hand and said, "Christie, I know your story, and I promise you, I am not that guy. Whoever hurt you—I promise you I am not him."

Feeling somewhat foolish and extremely self-conscious, Christie replied, "I just don't know if I can trust you. I want to, but at the same time I'm afraid."

"I know," he said. "But I've never given you any reason not to trust me. The real issue now is whether *I* can trust *you*, now that I know you've searched my wallet." The night was over.

Christie didn't hear from Bruce for three days. She wanted to call him, but she didn't. When he did call, she expected him to act like nothing had happened—that was how all her exes had behaved. But his actions confirmed that, just as he said, he was "not that guy." He asked to meet so they could discuss what had happened and where they could go from here. He got right to it. The card was in his ex's name. They were still good friends so they shared the account; he paid his portion, and she paid hers. That was all there was to it. As he described it, he had been lazy about getting the card transferred into his name, and it was a way to show that there were no ill feelings between them. The account was six years old, and they had never had a problem.

Bruce said that the real issue for him was the violation of his boundaries and Christie's lack of trust. He did not want to move forward in a relationship with a woman who did not trust him, even after he had demonstrated that he was trustworthy. He had nothing to hide, but he did not like having been searched and interrogated. He liked her a lot and wanted so much more for them, but Christie had crossed a line, and he didn't believe he could get beyond that.

Christie apologized and said she understood. She explained the mistake had stemmed from her fear, and she assured him it would never happen again. She asked for his forgiveness and wondered if they could try again. Bruce listened, accepted her apology, and told her he would have to get back to her. With that, he left enough money to pay for their drinks, kissed her on the cheek, and departed.

Christie was stunned and just a wee bit pissed off. One mistake! One stupid mistake and this was how he responded! WTF! If she meant so much to him, why couldn't they just move on? If she was that disposable, he must be up to something. If he was that unforgiving, maybe she didn't want him. Resigned to wait and see, Christie went home, where she wept for the next two weeks.

Moving from shock to anger to total denial, Christie waited a respectable month before she called Bruce. To her surprise, he picked up on the second ring. His voice was calm—as calm as usual. She thought that was a good sign. He was fine. He had been thinking about her and had just been waiting to be as clear as possible before contacting her. Boundaries, honesty, and trust were important to him. He understood where she was coming from, and it was not a place where he wanted to live. His concern was, what would be next? He had done everything in his power to be a demonstration of what he believed and of how he lived his life. Yet her behavior was an indication that she wasn't ready, and he wasn't willing to endure whatever might come along with her getting ready. No hard feelings. She was a beautiful woman. He had enjoyed their time together, but the relationship was not going to work for him. Without so much as a word in reply, Christie hung up.

The next three months were nothing short of brutal. Christie didn't understand how Bruce could be so direct and uncaring. Seven months together and he cut her off just like that? Where was his compassion? His understanding? Most of Christie's girlfriends agreed, but there was one—there's always one who tries to make sense out of the incomprehensible—who saw things differently. Angie suggested they apply the 4A's to the situation. She helped Christie to become aware of and acknowledge how her own thoughts had led her to search Bruce's wallet. It had been totally uncalled for, and it had been a violation of his boundaries. Obviously, Bruce was a man of integrity—an honest man who held a line on what was and was not acceptable. He had given her no reason to be suspicious. It was Christie's fear of repeating old patterns that had prompted her to make that move. Bruce's ending the relationship was his way of taking steps to protect himself, just as Christie had taken steps when she thought she needed to be protected from him.

At first, Christie just couldn't see it. It took many conversations before she bumped into her dominant negative thought patterns: "men cannot be trusted" and she "would never find the right guy." Once she acknowledged her DNTPs, she could finally admit how crazy she had been—being so brutally honest with herself wasn't easy. She admitted she'd always been listening for some contradiction, always been waiting for him to break a promise. She had even stalked his apartment twice, waiting to see if he came home alone. After several discussions with her posse, Christie admitted and accepted that she had expected Bruce to behave badly, and when he didn't, she did. OMG!

There was nothing to do, they said, beyond recognizing her fears and working to do better next time. What if there was no "next time"? What if she had blown the best thing that would ever happen for her? Angie, her reasonable, rational friend, assured her that life doesn't work like that. Life is a learn-as-you-go process. As we learn, we do better. Bruce had made his decision, and it would be foolish and too risky for her to try to convince him to change his mind. Acknowledging and accepting the error of her ways would open new doors for her. Forgiving herself would help her to avoid making the same mistakes in the future. It wasn't wrong to be cautious, but she also had to pay attention to the actual signs she received. Life provides an endless supply of do-overs. If you mess up the first time, you'll get another chance. Angie assured Christie that if she continued to do her work, moving through the fear, cleaning up her thoughts and expectations, things would change.

In the moment, it was hard for Christie to take it all in. She blamed herself and beat herself up and down for another three months. Finally, she moved into a state of acceptance. It was over and done. She wished Bruce well. She even decided to send him a thank-you note, expressing her gratitude to him for showing her the importance of trust and for holding his boundaries with such strength and clarity. She told him that she was doing fine and that she wished him well. Two weeks later, he called and asked if she would meet him at happy hour. He thought that maybe they could start fresh.

YOU MUST DO THE WORK

Christie's friend Angie had walked her through the 4A's process, explaining that the 4A's are the foundation of one's A game. Functioning as a kind of get-over-it jujitsu, they allow you to disarm your immediate experience rapidly so that you will become aware of and identify the roots of your DNTPs. For Christie, Bruce triggered the file of past relationships and the negative experiences that she dreaded. Remember, we are much more prone to recall our negative experiences than our positive ones. They send a stronger energetic sensation or feeling through the body. While these are the experiences we want desperately to avoid, we unwittingly rehearse them mentally. By thinking about what we don't want or what we will not do, in effect we deepen the emotional and psychological impressions that exist and, in turn, open one of the file drawers in our mind. The mental rehearsal—the constant rehashing of the meanings we have given to past thoughts, feelings, and experiences—is what adds ever more data to those bulging negative files. Then, when an extraordinarily new and fearful thought triggers us, we are left spinning in extreme emotional distress and overreaction—like going through someone's wallet when he's asleep.

That Angie was a very wise woman. She was able to help Christie recognize her own thoughts and feelings that had nothing to do with Bruce. That awareness was a giant step forward for Christie. Then, by acknowledging and accepting the truth about her own behaviors and overreactions, Christie demonstrated her willingness to have a new experience. Finally, by engaging in the completely loving action of forgiving herself and expressing gratitude toward Bruce, Christie, in effect, freed her mind from her hidden DNTPs. There can be no doubt that this breakthrough left Ms. Claudie beaming.

CHAPTER 3

TROUBLED MINDS: A FAMILY HISTORY

Every thought you produce, anything you say,
any action you do, it bears your signature.

—THICH NHAT HANH

W hat you think and how you think are not private matters. Since thoughts determine how we approach and respond to life, everyone in our sphere will become familiar with the state of our mind. The people we spend the most time with will come to learn our likes and dislikes, our propensities, and our probable responses in many given situations. Statements such as "You know how she is" or "You know he's not going to like that" are, in essence, testimonies given by our loved ones that indicate just how aware they are of our habitual patterns of thought. Our dominant thought patterns tell people a lot about us, and our thought patterns often determine how others behave around us. More important, how those people around us think—that is, their dominant negative thought patterns—will also have a definite impact on us.

BLOOD LINE EQUALS A LINE OF THOUGHTS

Some of us grew up in families and environments that were desperately dysfunctional and emotionally destructive. This was the case with Allen. He is the son of a 16-year-old high school student with a slight learning disability and a 17-year-old high school dropout. Allen's mother, Rose, lived with her mother, Annie Brown, who herself had been a teenage mother. Allen's birth brought to life and light an entrenched generational family history of dominant negative thought patterns and the results that follow when an entire family remains unconscious of them.

Rose was never a "little girl." At age 16, she stood 5 feet 9 inches tall and carried about 50 extra pounds. So it didn't seem at all odd that she wore her clothing extra-large to hide her "fluffy" stomach. Rose hid her fluffy stomach pregnancy well because she was terrified of her mother's reaction.

When Annie decided to take her daughter to Planned Parenthood for birth control, it didn't seem unusual. In Annie's mind, she was doing for her daughter what no one had done for her. She knew that young girls who grew up in fatherless households faced terrible temptations, and she wanted to protect Rose from the potential result of giving in to those temptations: an unwanted pregnancy. As a cautious and realistic parent, Annie knew that her many lectures to Rose about no sex and safe sex would mean very little when her daughter encountered seductive propositions from the neighborhood boys. She was determined that Rose wouldn't repeat her history. The day of their appointment at Planned Parenthood, however, Annie learned that Rose was already 35 weeks pregnant.

The soon-to-be grandmother and mother-to-be were living in a friend's house, where Annie, who was unemployed at the time, was scrambling to pay weekly rent and buy food. Annie's older daughter, Bev, a college freshman with very little financial support, was also part of the struggling extended family. Bev had made it through her first two semesters of college by charging other students a small fee to braid their hair. When that was no longer sufficient to sustain her, Bev dropped out of college, returned home, and got a job at McDonald's. She had learned from her mother, Annie, that you do whatever you have to do to take care of those you love, even when it means putting your own dreams on hold.

An unplanned pregnancy and another mouth to feed were the last things the Brown family needed. In this family, "there's never enough" was not only a dominant negative thought pattern in everyone's mental files, it was also a physical reality. Needless to say, after the revelation of Rose's condition at Planned Parenthood, Annie *lost* it. It wasn't so much the screaming and swearing that impacted Rose, it was Annie's relentless shaming and belittling of her terrified daughter that deepened in Rose's brain the DNTP imprints and the family patterns of guilt, fear, and humiliation. And Annie wasn't reacting so much to the knowledge that Rose had been sexually active, Annie was livid that Rose had lied to her, covered up her pregnancy for months, and put the entire family in jeopardy. This was exactly what Annie had felt when she had been pregnant and abandoned as a 16-year-old.

Annie was so upset. Did Rose feel the baby moving? Did she understand the importance of prenatal care? They had no medical coverage. The earliest prenatal appointment Annie could get for Rose was two weeks out. What did Rose mean that "she didn't want to be on welfare"? And who was the father? Where was he? Thank God, he wasn't the son of one of the neighbors! Annie offered her pregnant daughter no compassion, no support, no guidance, and no counseling. Rose's mind and the atmosphere in the household were thick with an overabundance of emotional abandonment and absolute, uncontrollable rage during her son's womb time. Welcome to the world, baby boy!

Allen was born two weeks and two days after the family discovered that Rose was pregnant. On Memorial Day that year, after 23 hours of labor, Allen made his appearance: 6 pounds 19 ounces, 19 inches long. Mother, grandmother, and auntie welcomed Allen with kisses and prayers. He was a beautiful baby! Family friends made sure he had everything he needed, from diapers to a stroller, from a high chair to a used bassinet. Although receiving those items for Allen was a blessing, both Rose and Annie felt embarrassed to need anything from anyone. Allen's formula was made the old-fashioned way, with evaporated milk and Karo syrup in a sterilizer. It wasn't the optimal choice, but the family had a history of making do with what they had and not expecting more. Allen wore cloth diapers because Pampers weren't even on the market in poor neighborhoods at that time. Rose eventually shared her baby daddy's name with her mother, but mysteriously he could not be located, not even after Annie contacted the school. No such student had ever been enrolled. Annie wasn't surprised: she had grown up in a family where the men had *always* disappeared when they were needed.

Annie was adamant that Rose should complete her junior year of high school. So Rose spent the first two weeks after the birth at home with her new baby, then resumed classes. In her absence, Auntie Bev became Allen's primary caregiver. While Rose did her homework, Grandma and Auntie shared the childcare duties. And at every opportunity Grandma pointed out to Rose what she needed to be doing, what she wasn't doing, and what she shouldn't be doing as far as baby Allen was concerned. Annie's constant corrections and criticisms were the manifestation of a multigenerational pattern related to parental irresponsibility, personal inferiority, and the inadequacy of women within the Brown family.

Nighttime in the Brown household made it clear to everyone that a serious problem was brewing between mother and son. The fear, shame, and guilt surrounding her pregnancy ordeal had made bonding with Allen impossible for Rose. She would let her son cry for hours, or until his auntie came to rescue him. Annie would lie awake in her bed, pretending she didn't hear her grandbaby crying or her daughters arguing. It wasn't a new experience for her. She had learned how to do that— ignore what was going on around her—in her childhood home, where domestic violence had been an everyday affair.

Allen's cries for attention and nurturing must have triggered memories from his womb time. His mother's painful emotional experiences during his formative development— when his very existence had been a terrible secret—had riddled his energy system with holes. It's not easy being a pregnant teenager under any circumstances. However, when the young mother is tormented by fear, guilt, and shame, an unplanned pregnancy can only escalate her incredibly vulnerable state of mind and being. Rose had no support during her pregnancy—a time of significant hormonal, physiological, and psychological shifts in a woman's being. Along with the weight gain, mood swings, physical cravings, and discomforts, Rose had been consumed with negative thoughts and feelings designed to keep two people in hiding rather than just one.

SOME STUFF . . . YOU BRING IN WITH YOU

In the case of an expected pregnancy, preparations are made for the baby as well as for the life of the future family. There is also, hopefully, some joy and excitement surrounding the promise of a new life. Yet in Allen's case, and the case of so many others, there was no planning or welcome. Assaulted by a myriad of toxic emotions and generational poverty, Allen started life behind the eight ball. In the womb, he took on the physiological, psychological, and emotional experiences of his mother. These "direct hits" landed like energetic bombs and were deeply imprinted into the fibers his being.

Scientific research has confirmed that a woman's nutritional condition, psychological states, and emotional propensities do in fact influence the predispositions of the children she gives birth to. Such susceptibilities often manifest as low self-esteem, a diminished state of self-value, and a lack of self-worth later in life. Allen gestated in a toxic womb and was born into a physically and psychologically stressed environment.

The deck was stacked against him. It would be a real toss-up, though, to decide which was worse—what happened before he was born, or what happened once he came into life.

When Allen was two, Grandma Annie moved to a new state and took her grandson with her. Annie's plan was to give Rose the opportunity to finish training as a nursing assistant. Once she completed the program, Rose would join her mother and gain certification in their new town. Rose stayed with a family friend, attended classes, and, within a year, found herself pregnant again. Allen's brother, Jackson, was born under circumstances similar to Allen's birth; he was hidden from his mother's side of the family. (However, he was known about and welcomed by his father's side of the family.) Allen was only eight days shy of turning three when his half-brother was born.

Although Annie's work and financial situation had changed dramatically during those years, she refused to take on the responsibility of another child. Rose and Jackson visited Annie, Bev, and Allen three or four times a year, but Rose rarely, if ever, called to check in on her firstborn. Allen considered his Auntie Bev to be his mom. She was the one who nurtured him, took him to the park, and helped him with his homework. When he did, on rare occasions, ask why he couldn't live with his mother and brother, the answers he received were vague.

By the time Allen was seven, he would cry, "My mother loves Jackson but not me!" and "Where is my father? Jackson has a father—how come I don't have one?" Grandma Annie did her best to explain, but the truth was, she had no idea who Allen's father was or where he was. When Allen started having problems in school, he said that because "he was a throwaway," his mother didn't want him or love him. By the first time he was suspended from school, for the first time, he said he didn't care about his mom or his brother not loving him. "All I want is my father," he cried.

It was Christmastime at Grandma's house. Everybody was there trimming the tree, wrapping presents, and anticipating the huge holiday dinner. Allen slept in his room; his mother and brother, who were visiting, slept in the guest room. Auntie Bev and her daughter, as well as Allen's uncle Jack, traveled back and forth to Grandma's house because they lived locally. On Christmas Eve morning, Grandma Annie heard Rose moving around in the kitchen and could smell breakfast being prepared, so she took the opportunity to sleep in.

Later, when Annie came downstairs, she found Allen alone at the kitchen table eating cereal. She asked why he hadn't eaten earlier. Allen explained that his mother had prepared bacon and eggs for herself and his brother, but that she had told him he couldn't have any and would have to wait for his grandma to give him his breakfast.

Upon hearing Allen's account and seeing the look on his face, Grandma put her foot down with Rose hard and swift, informing her that this was Allen's home and no one entering had the right to deny him food. In addition, because Rose was his mother, whether or not she was raising him, her first priority was to ensure that her son's needs were met. Rose, on the defensive, claimed that she didn't know what Allen liked, and blah-blah-blah. That tense exchange set the tone for the entire day. Feuding during holiday gatherings was another family pattern that Annie had lived through as a child and then unwittingly passed on to her children. When they were all together, the Brown family members said and did the most outrageous things to express their pent-up anger.

By the time the tree was trimmed, Annie had informed both Uncle Jack and Auntie Bev about the morning's events. Everyone had his or her take on the situation, and no one knew what to say to Allen. Rose seemed embarrassed, ashamed, and angry that she had been called out, yet she still felt justified in her actions. To give everyone some breathing space and perhaps create a little peace, Uncle Jack decided to make the final run to the store. He invited Rose, Allen, and Jackson to join him. As Annie heard the story, Allen and his brother were in the back seat, Jack was driving, and Rose was riding shotgun. Just the way little boys will do, Allen was teasing his younger brother, and Jackson didn't like it. He ratted on him, saying something like, "Mom, Allen keeps bothering me."

Without offering any instruction or issuing a command, Rose turned around in her seat, reached back, and punched her son Allen dead in the face. In response, Allen grabbed his mother by the hair and began to pummel her. At nine years old, Allen had experienced the first of what would be many physical altercations with his mother. Uncle Jack had to stop the car to separate them. Standing in the snow along the side of the road, Uncle Jack delivered a long lecture to both of them. He then put Allen in the front seat, and Rose moved to the back seat with Jackson. They never made it to the store. Upon their return home, after hearing the various reports of what had happened, Annie gave Rose and Jackson their presents and instructed Uncle Jack to take them to his home.

Grandma spent hours trying her best to answer Allen's questions about why his mother would treat him that way. He was heartbroken. Since there was no explanation she could offer that made any sense, Annie just held her grandson as he cried. Being physically and emotionally abandoned, feeling unworthy of his mother's love, Allen felt helpless. It wasn't until the day after Christmas that he finally came down to open his gifts; by then, everyone else had gone. It would be almost a year before Allen saw or spoke to his mother again.

THE APPLE AND THE TREE

If the young Allen had been aware of the concept of DNTPs, he would have been able to understand how the sensations in which he'd marinated during his womb time had been transmitted from his mother to him. During her pregnancy, Rose had felt afraid, guilty, and alone. It's a pretty safe bet that she spent most of those months wondering why Allen's father had abandoned her, how she could make things right with her mother, and whether or not she even wanted the baby that she was carrying. All of these feelings also generated a pretty generous dose of "why me" anger. Added to the normal stresses of being 16 years old and brokenhearted, it's no wonder that Allen, from the get-go, developed the sense of being unloved, unwanted, and unworthy, even though those feelings had nothing to do with him.

Allen had steeped in his mother's guilt, dishonesty, and shame—it's all about energy. A helplessness file had been created within him before he was born. We can imagine that Rose cried many nights, feeling alone, afraid, and totally incapable of fulfilling her duties as a mother. When Allen cried, she couldn't soothe him because she hadn't been soothed or supported when she had needed it most. Children learn early, during the first three years of their lives, whether they can trust that they will be cared for and whether they are safe. Rose's stressful emotional state became Allen's womb-time reality. With no explanation or understanding of his mother's personal history or the generational inheritances, that he was unworthy of love was the only explanation Allen could come up with. These files became the foundation of Allen's dominant negative thought patterns.

As a child, an adolescent, and eventually as a young man, any time Allen had a thought that triggered a sensation that was familiar, he was filled with shame and guilt and unworthiness. The common internal dialogue most often associated with these feelings are these: "I don't matter!" "Something is wrong with me!" "Something is wrong with what I've done!" "Why bother?!" Processing these DNTPs results in unexplained anger that eventually seeps out as rage. Every thought that triggered these all-too-familiar sensations that Allen inherited from his mother meant that his dominant negative thought files just grew and grew. When our emotional files grow so big that they start to overwhelm our capacity to understand the thoughts we think and the feelings we have, they lead to behaviors that become our undiagnosed traumas.

ONE THING ON TOP OF ANOTHER

When Allen was 12 years old, his Auntie Bev—the woman he called his mother—died. His grandmother, Annie, was bedridden from the emotional despair following the loss of her daughter. Although she tried to keep Allen's life moving forward, Grandma Annie had no physical or emotional energy to offer her grandson. Auntie Bev was gone, and Allen felt abandoned once again. Rose mothered his half-brother Jackson, but she wasn't willing to do the same for Allen. Everything had changed in his world as a result of Bev's death, and no one knew what to do or say about it. So Allen made up that he was worthless and couldn't do anything about his situation. Allen's helplessness was a familiar open file, and his rage file was developing in the same way.

For the first four months after Auntie Bev's death, Allen was on his own . . . again. Family friends came by to check on Grandma and make sure he was okay, but after doing his homework, he usually ate and watched television alone. However, by the fourth time Allen was suspended from school, Grandma Annie knew that she had to do something different.

Annie eventually took a job out of state, hoping to avoid the painful memories and to move forward in her own life. She decided to enroll Allen in a boarding school, where he would have structure and discipline and be in the company of men who could support and guide him. Annie explained to Allen that she would be able to visit and that she would arrange her schedule to accommodate his school holidays. Things seemed to be going well until she got a call from the school.

Two months into his first term, Allen was involved in a physical altercation with another student who had said something Allen didn't like. Since the school had a zero tolerance policy for physical violence, they recommended that Allen be transferred to another facility that could accommodate a "troubled youth" who acted out.

Allen told Annie he had felt justified in defending himself against the other student's verbal assaults. (Defending herself during her pregnancy against Annie's verbal tirades was something Rose had been unable to do.) But he was sorry for causing such a problem. (Annie had often told her own mother the same thing when she was a teenager.) Allen just wanted to come home. Grandma Annie explained that she would be working on the West Coast for another five months and that doing so was the only way she could afford to advance her career, qualify for a big raise, and continue to take care of him. She asked Allen to try out the new school she had found. If it didn't work, she would bring him home. After learning that the new school was in Jamaica, Allen finally conceded.

The new school, after conducting several tests and counseling sessions, determined that Allen not only had a learning disability, he most probably had Attention Deficit Hyperactivity Disorder (ADHD). According to his counselor, Allen often did not sleep for two or three days at a time. He would walk the floor all night. Reluctantly, Annie agreed that he could be medicated, but only to help him with sleeping. (It was only a fleeting thought, but Annie remembered how Rose had experienced a similar sleeplessness during her pregnancy.) Allen's late-night agitation disturbed the other boys and was beginning to affect his performance in class. In spite of everything, his grades were pretty good: ranging from an A– to a B+.

Everyone agreed that Allen was very intelligent and capable, but his defiant behavior kept sabotaging everything. The school operated on a point system, and because of his rebellion against authority and aggressiveness toward the other students, Allen rarely rose above Level 1. When he finally did reach Level 3, he lost the points within 24 hours because of a fight. Despite the fact that Allen had lost his visitation privileges, Annie boarded a plane for Jamaica, informing the school that if she was not allowed to see her grandson, it was her intention to shut the place down!

When Annie arrived in Jamaica, she hadn't seen Allen in five months and had spoken to him only twice. He was constantly on restriction, which meant he had no visitation or telephone privileges. Allen looked fine. He was much taller; his voice had deepened, and he had a few straggly hairs above his upper lip and on his chin. His baby face still didn't look a day over 12, but he was now 16. Annie's first concern was his slightly slurred speech. Allen explained it was a side effect of his medication, which also made him sluggish and sleepy.

Allen's grades were still good, and his homeroom teacher confirmed that he definitely had college potential. The big problem was his behavior. He was disrespectful to all adults, particularly women. Hearing this, Annie knew immediately that this was a reflection of his relationship with his mother. Rose's behavior toward her son had left him heartbroken many times over, and because he didn't understand it, he was angry. In addition, the teacher continued, Allen was both defensive and aggressive with men. Annie had learned this was a common experience among fatherless sons. Also, he had no coping skills when it came to dealing with his peers. More often than not, Allen was the first one to throw a punch. When that happened, his teacher explained, he refused to accept responsibility for his behavior. He was always the victim: someone had glared at him, or had said something to him, or had approached him the wrong way. When he wasn't fighting, he isolated. There were days he had to be forced to eat. There were nights when he still did not sleep. But even through all of this, everyone at the school liked Allen. His teachers recognized that he was a good but deeply troubled kid. During a conversation, Allen made one statement to Annie that shattered her heart, sending her to the airport and back home in primal pain. Allen said, "I really do try, Grandma, but I just don't understand why nobody wants me. Even you—you keep sending me away." Forty-eight hours after that conversation, Annie had Allen flown back to the United States.

At first, Allen seemed sullen and somewhat disconnected after his return, not only from himself but also from everyone and everything. Annie recognized that this was exactly the way Rose had behaved after Allen was born. Finally, Allen enrolled in a new school run by a husband-and-wife team who clearly loved and knew how to inspire young people while teaching them responsibility and accountability. There, Allen seemed to get back on track. He graduated from high school and even got a leadership award.

After commencement, Allen attended community college and was studying to become a veterinary assistant. Unable to find a job to support himself, he decided to enlist in the Navy. But following three physical altercations, Allen was granted a general discharge and advised to seek counseling for anger management. He had been home for three weeks before he told his grandmother what had happened.

Allen admitted that he felt both guilty and ashamed of himself but, again, justified in his behavior. Allen had been a "victim" of Rose's toxic emotions while in her womb, just as, while pregnant, Rose had been a victim of Annie's verbal and emotional assaults. Allen had no tools or defenses against his mother, his extended family, or his environment. This is exactly what his mother had experienced. As a young boy, he started building his own files: "I can't help it . . . I'm alone . . . It's my fault . . . I don't matter." Allen said he hated having people in his face. Rose didn't like it, either, when she experienced it with her mother.

Although Allen told his grandmother that he was living with a friend and working on a construction site, neither was true. He lied to protect himself and to defend against the verbal assault he expected to endure if he told Annie where he was really staying.

The truth was, Allen had moved in with Rose and Jackson, in Rose's one-bedroom apartment. Being near his mother was something Allen had yearned for all his life. He and his brother slept on the pullout sofa. These living arrangements came to light only after Allen and his mother had a physical altercation and she called the police. Allen's brother, Jackson, called Annie, hoping that she could calm them both down so Allen wouldn't be arrested. Unfortunately, the police officers did not take kindly to Allen swearing at them and refusing to leave when they asked him to do so. Allen insisted that his mother was the one who should be arrested because she had used his toothpaste and lied about it. This on top of her accusing him of drinking her soda when he had not. When certain emotional files are congested, dominant negative thought patterns will make little things, small slights, seem huge. After spending three days in jail, Allen moved back to his grandmother's house. He was 20 years old.

LEARNING AND EARNING SELF-LOVE

By the time Annie introduced me to her grandson Allen, he had no hope for himself or his life. When children get the womb-time message that they are unwanted or unwelcome, they often have a difficult time finding their way in life. "Why bother?" is a common dominant negative thought pattern for these souls. During several of our conversations, when Allen became emotionally overwrought, he wished himself dead and threatened to give up on everyone and everything. I suspected he also learned this despair in the womb. Allen was beyond angry; he was enraged. He was also depressed, desperate, and despondent. He accepted no ownership or responsibility for his current life experience. Instead, he was stuck in his dominant negative thoughts of "I don't matter" and "Nobody wants me."

When following up with Annie, I explained that Allen's hopelessness was my major concern. Without hope, a person cannot muster up the strength or courage to take the next most appropriate steps. I told Annie that I would work with her grandson, but I wouldn't accept any form of payment. I would act as a coach—not a therapist. Sometimes it's best for a person to work with a therapist, in order to unpack the past; other times it's better to work with a coach, in order to design and create a productive future. I agreed to work with Allen because I respected his grandmother, and I could hear something in Allen's voice that indicated that he could be turned toward a new direction.

I understood that Allen's healing work had deep generational roots. In my conversations with Annie, I could hear several dominant negative thought patterns that I was sure Allen had picked up along the way. Every once in a while, Allen would say, "I just don't understand why I'm like this. I really, really try. I can do everything right for a while, and then something happens that reminds me that nobody wants me and nobody loves me." Most people are unaware that they have dominant negative thought patterns and become frustrated trying to unravel the behaviors these patterns evoke.

When I reminded Allen of how much his grandmother loves and supports him, he would quietly reply, "Yeah, but she sent me away, too. Just like my mother." When I pointed out that they both had done the best they could, he said, "Yeah, they did. They threw out the trash. I'm their trash." If we do not understand the energy that spills forth from our subconscious mental and emotional files, we turn what we think and feel into self-destructive beliefs.

While it broke my heart to hear Allen speak of himself as "trash," I also realized that he had been capsized by his dominant negative thought patterns—they were destroying his capacity to create a productive and meaningful life. Some of his patterns were inherited. Others he had created himself. Children inherently believe they will be safe in the presence of those who care for them. Any psychologist worth her weight will tell you that the most damaging and debilitating betrayal a child can experience is betrayal by one or both parents. What I knew and believed with all of my soul was this: if Allen could become willing to change, he would be able to change. It would take some time, but it was possible. It would require my supporting Allen in sorting through his thoughts and feelings and choosing how to respond. It also meant teaching Allen how to circumvent certain thoughts and feelings by installing new ones.

SILENT IS THE POWER OF THOUGHT

Allen inherited much of his rage. His experiences of helplessness, hopelessness, and worthlessness were likely outgrowths of his mother's dominant negative thought patterns. Like his mother, Allen felt trapped by the circumstances of his life and victimized by the ways those in his environment responded to their experience. Allen's DNTPs impacted his ability and capacity to make conscious choices and decisions when certain feelings were triggered. Allen fought against what he was feeling by fighting other people. His behavior was undoubtedly a misguided attempt and a futile choice to protect himself. The key word in all of this is "choice." We all have to navigate the psychological and emotional pathology we inherit from our parents and environment; however, nothing we experience eliminates our free will and our ability to choose how to respond. As we grow and mature, there comes a moment when we must examine the choices we make and the consequences of those choices. These alone are our responsibility.

✦

**What you think
becomes what you believe.**

**What you believe
determines how you behave.**

**How you behave
determines what you experience.**

✦

Getting Allen to understand that his thoughts were powerful and that he was not a victim or worthless was more than a challenge. His "stuff" was so etched into the fibers of his being and integrated into his physical world experience, he could not hear or accept much of what I said to him. Then one day I made a comment that gave us both a glimmer of hope. It was one of my favorite lessons from *A Course in Miracles*.

"Allen, there is nothing that your holiness cannot do."

"Holiness? What does that mean? I ain't holy."

"Yes, you are holy and divine and loved."

"What makes me holy?"

"Your breathing makes you holy. The power of your mind makes you holy."

"Can my breathing or the power of my mind make my mother love me or help me find my father?"

"No. But your holiness and your belief in it can give you enough strength so that not having either of those things won't stop you from being holy."

"Okay then. Show me how to do that."

I gave Allen the affirmation of Psalm 27, verse 10, *Even if my father and mother abandon me, the Lord will take care of me.* He didn't really understand the concept of the Lord, so I told him that how you think and what you think constitutes the Lord of your life. From a spiritual perspective, the Lord is the law; it governs what you do and how you do it. Allen and I worked with this one affirmation to combat his thoughts and feelings about shame, guilt, and unworthiness. Although he didn't fully grasp the concept, he entertained the notion that being "taken care of" and loved by a power greater than himself, outside of himself, could mean that he and his life actually did matter.

After working with Allen over the course of a year, one day he arrived at my office wearing a bright green T-shirt. On the front of it were these words:

THERE IS NOTHING
MY HOLINESS CANNOT DO.

We had a wonderful conversation that day, and he told me that he had once more enrolled in community college to complete his studies so he could become a veterinary assistant. After he left, I wept.

PART II
THOUGHT THERAPY

CHAPTER 4

THE GET OVER IT!
(GOI) TOOLS

You are today where your thoughts have brought you;
you will be tomorrow where your thoughts take you.

—JAMES ALLEN

W hen I was growing up, no one taught me anything about personal finances or money management. I heard the adults in my life complain about paying bills, and I watched them struggle to get them paid. Their complaints were often accompanied by angry arguments, feelings of frustration, and the temporary elimination of essential needs or services, such as electricity, gas, telephone, and in some cases, shelter. Although everyone was engaged in some sort of income-generating activity, a lot of drama always surrounded bill paying, and there never seemed to be enough money to pay them at all, let alone pay them on time. As a child, I was deprived of many things—including some meals—because something was due that required the reallocation of food money. I grew up with a fear of bills and a total disregard for when, if, and how I paid them.

By the time my children and I were being evicted from our third apartment for the nonpayment of rent, I realized that I simply had to do better. At the time, I did not have the depth of spiritual commitment that I have today; however, I knew how to pray. I had 48 hours to pay the rent in order to stop the city marshal from putting my children, my furniture, and me out on the street. Addressing this situation required an old-fashioned, down-on-your-knees, affirming-God's-glory kind of prayer. That is exactly what I did.

I started by acknowledging who and what I believed God to be in my life. Then, as my grandmother had taught me, I confessed my role in the situation. I confessed my own fiscal irresponsibility. I confessed my negligence and resistance as it related to how I spent money. I remember taking a few liberties with Psalm 23, one of my favorite chapters of scripture. I prayed something like this: *Yea, though my parents were poor and negligent about paying their bills, I want to be different. I want to live better. I shall not fear being evicted. I shall not fear not having enough money to provide for my children. For I know you are with me, God, and no harm shall come near me or my house. Your grace and your mercy now cover me and my home. Lead me to do things the right way. Help me to do it.*

I prayed for a very long time. I was not begging or pleading for mercy. I was asking for what I needed, and I believed I could have it. I asked for the money, of course, but I also realized that I had had the money and had misallocated it. I asked for more time to gather the money. I asked to be led to the person who could loan me the money. I even asked to be led where to go if it was God's will and my just rewards that I be evicted. Then I asked for a miracle that would keep my children and me safe. By the time I finished praying, I was exhausted, and I was at peace.

The next morning, I woke up with what's called "a leading." I got dressed, fed the children, and dropped them off with a neighbor, promising to bring her back two Pepsi Colas and a sour pickle. I went straight to Housing Court. When I arrived, there was no line—miracle number one. I asked the clerk there how to file a stay and an appeal to an order of eviction. She asked me if I had children. Yes, three. She asked me if I was working. No, I received public assistance. Then miracle number two happened. The clerk informed me that I should not be in court, I should go to the public assistance office and ask for an emergency housing grant to avoid eviction. She told me I was entitled to two a year for extreme circumstances. She asked me if I had been through any extreme circumstances, such as a death in the family that had required out-of-state travel, domestic violence that had required a hotel stay, or a burglary that had required the replacement of windows or locks. These things, she told me, would require expenditures not covered by my public assistance budget.

Unfortunately, none of those situations applied to me. When I told her that, she looked at me with one eyebrow raised. I knew what that meant; however, I also knew that I could not expect divine intervention if I was telling a lie. I was thinking out loud when I told her that I had lived for nine years in an abusive relationship but that it had ended about a year earlier. As if she knew what I was thinking, she reached across the counter, tapped me on the shoulder, and said, "They don't ask you *when* it happened, they ask you *if* it happened." Then she said, "You don't have to say it, you only have to write it down on the form. That should be enough to get the ball rolling."

In an instant, the same peaceful feeling I'd had after I made my prayer came over me again. Although I understood that everything hadn't been resolved at that moment, God had led me to my next best step. As I turned to leave, the clerk reminded me, "Be sure to tell them to call the marshal even before they give you the check."

By 4:30 that afternoon, I had in my hands a check to cover my back rent plus two Pepsis and a sour pickle for my neighbor. This was my first awareness that heartfelt and earnest prayer could change something *within*. This experience opened me up to believing and feeling differently about what was possible and how I could step into that possibility. I lived in that apartment for another two years and never again had a late rent payment.

MASTERING YOUR MIND

Repetition is the mother of skill. The more you do something, the better you become at executing or performing whatever you are doing. Athletes and dancers call it practice. Students call it study. No matter who is doing it or what it's called, most of us hate the process of doing the same thing over and over. Unfortunately, it is the way, the *only* way, to develop a skill or master a craft. Repetition, practice, study is how to develop muscle, stamina, and mastery that will move you toward the realization of your pursuit. The Get Over It! thought therapy work you are about to embark upon is geared toward developing mental muscles, emotional stamina, and the skills required to master your mind.

I don't know much about golf. In fact, I find it to be quite boring. As an uneducated onlooker, it seems to me that you're required to hit a ball with a stick with the intention of making it go in a hole, one that's located very far away from where you and the stick are. One day I let a friend talk me into going to a mini golf course to have some fun. I agreed, but I was thinking, *What kind of fun is it to knock a ball into a hole with a stick?*

During the entire ride to the course, she tried to convince me that golf was about so much more. I didn't believe her. But since I had nothing better to do, I was along partially for the ride, partially for the promise of a good meal afterward. I will do almost anything for food. On the way to the mini course, we passed a real golf course, and my friend suggested that we go for the hell of it.

Once we got our shoes, we had to select our clubs. Once that was done, and we had our balls, we went out to the course and the real fun began. I won't bore you with the details about how I stood in the sun for hours, following my friend's very specific instructions and feeling the sweat trickling down my back, yet never got even one of my balls near a hole. My balls ended up in the bushes, on the other side of a fence, or completely lost, never to be found. I absolutely did not have fun, but I learned a great deal about golf, myself, and how the mind works.

My friend must have repeated at least 500 times three key words—balance, grip, and tempo—but I just couldn't get the hang of it. Balance refers to how you stand or plant your feet; grip means how you hold the club; tempo reflects the back swing, the forward swing, and the pivoting of the body you are trying to keep balanced while swinging the club in order to hit the ball. I am telling you, it was a long, hot day! I never came close to mastering balance, grip, and tempo on that day, nor do I think they are essential to my life or my happiness. It was, however, the other stuff she said about golf that kept me out there in the sun.

She told me that golf is a mental game as much as it is a physical one, and she talked about awareness—staying aware of your body, aware of how it feels and how it moves. Tension in the body or the mind, she explained, is a golf demon; it will send your ball straight to hell. Then she talked about focus and concentration. This, my friend explained, is essential for creating and maintaining control of the club. It's your mind that establishes a link between the club and the body and the hole.

It was only after I lost my fifth ball and my friend yelled at me in frustration that my mind abandoned its anticipation of eating dinner and became focused on the golf. The gist of what she said was this: I had to visualize how I wanted to hit the ball. I had to form a mental picture of where I wanted the ball to go. Then I had to allow my instincts to show me a target line: the path the ball would travel to the target hole.

In the meantime, I had to remain aware of my posture and make sure that I held that image in my mind as I hit the ball and completed my follow-through.

Then she said, "Now relax and hit the damn ball, please!" By that point, my mind was racing. I was so distracted by what she was saying that I maybe would have hit the ball had the club not flown out of my hands on the back swing. How many of us lose our focus and balance *in* life or our grip *on* life because of the dominant negative thought patterns in which we engage? How many more of us ignore, dismiss, or deny how we feel about ourselves and our life as a result of how we think? So much of what she told me about golf was easily and readily applicable to what we think and feel, and how our DNTPs affect the direction and condition of our lives.

On the way home, after a lovely Italian dinner, I kept thinking, *Repetition is the is the mother of skill, and what we focus on grows.* When we're not aware of what we're thinking, we're very likely to repeat to ourselves the same dominant negative thoughts until we master them. Many people do exactly this. They master these thoughts by believing them, even when they're not true: *You're so stupid! You never do anything right! You can't do that!*

Every negative belief about ourselves or every uncertainty about our ability to do something carries an energy that will open a DNTP file—a fear file, a guilt file, a why-bother file. Thoughts and beliefs feed expectations: "I'll never do it! I can't . . . It doesn't matter anyway." These thoughts are more often than not attached to outcomes we expect, whether or not our expectations are supported by reality. So very often we master thoughts, beliefs, and expectations about the very things we *don't* want because of the silent, terrifying, unconscious thoughts that we repeat in our mind.

Because the mind really does have a tendency to mull over negative experiences with greater detail than positive ones, examining and remembering experiences and stories of the past, whether our own or those of others, usually does not turn out well for us. Especially when we are attempting to create change or develop something different in our lives.

On the drive home from the restaurant that night, I recognized that if the unconscious dominant negative thought patterns had the power to hold us back, then surely positive conscious thoughts could move us forward.

Prayer and affirmations are conscious, positive, and productive thoughts that can close some negative files and create some positive ones. Further, the more we repeat positive thoughts, focusing on the productive and positive outcomes, the stronger the link will be between what we are thinking, doing, and experiencing. Who knew that a day on a golf course could bring about such life-changing revelations?

THE 5 GET OVER IT! (GOI) TOOLS

I. Thought Therapy Prayer

While the scriptures remind us, 'For we wrestle not against flesh and blood, but against principalities, against powers, against the rulers of the darkness of this world, against spiritual wickedness in high places,' few of us realize that the highest place in which we can dwell is our own mind.

—EMMET FOX, ON EPHESIANS 6:12

Today, almost all of us have a cell phone or other device that allows us to interact with one another. In many cases these devices have become a necessity in both our business and personal lives. We recognize the importance of being and staying connected. We want to talk and listen to those we care about, and we want them to hear from us.

Paradoxically, many people who routinely dial, post, text, and tweet friends and family around the world have failed to activate their free 24/7 direct access to the Divine. Why is that? This unhackable, uncensored communication medium that I'm referring to, this unsurpassed method of talking to God, Christ, Source, Higher Self, Spirit—or whatever name you use for the Divine—is prayer.

Prayer is the process of communication that allows each of us to turn within and connect with the Divine Spark, the presence of God that exists as the essence of our being. For the purposes of the GOI work in this book, I encourage you to consider that this Source is within you. So often we pray to an external entity or deity, and then we want and wait for something outside of ourselves to do something for us. Because we are endeavoring to transform the mind, it's important to turn within and create a connection to the source of your thoughts, beliefs, and expectations that ultimately influences your experiences. In a nutshell, prayer is the way and means by which we connect with God at the core of our being. It is like a person-to-person phone call to God—within the person who is making the call.

One of the most perfect forms of prayer proven to yield miraculous results is affirmative prayer. This form of spiritual petition focuses on a desired and positive outcome rather than a problem or negative situation. By affirming the desired intention as if it's already happened, affirmative prayer teaches us to program the mind about what to expect. Remember, expectations are beliefs that determine what we experience, and we always get what we expect. The process of affirmative prayer elevates the mind above the physical-world reality of time and space into the uncharted realm of limitless possibility. With the process of affirmative prayer in this proactive state of mind, we are shifting the energy within our own consciousness and creating a new energy imprint. The premise of affirmative prayer is that in order to create and experience that which we desire, we must first connect with it at the mental level. By using the very highest and best language at our command, affirmative prayers consciously weed out thoughts of failure, lack, and loss, as well as the toxic energy of dominant negative thought patterns. Affirmative prayer elevates our thinking and speaking. It plants in the fertile ground of our minds new seeds that will grow into a physical-world reality.

Each affirmative prayer offered for the GOI process addresses one of the 42 dominant negative thought patterns we will be working to heal and clear. With these prayers, you are not pleading, begging, or asking for anything. You are making clear and definitive statements that are designed to shift the energy of your consciousness in order to transform what you experience in your life. As your mental energy shifts, how you see yourself and how you feel about yourself and your life can and will change. New seeds of positive and productive energy will be planted in your thought process. As these seeds germinate and sprout, you'll experience a greater mental and emotional alignment with where you desire to be and how you can get there.

I encourage you to be mindful that prayer is not a magic wand. You can pray all you want, but you will still need to do the work required to make your dreams and intentions a reality. The good news is that through affirmative prayer you will be open to and will be able to see greater possibilities than before. In other words, you will be able to see the hole on the golf course and have some idea about the path your ball should follow to get into the hole. What prayer will do is balance the playing field by eliminating internal and, in some cases, external obstacles. It will also give you a firm mental grip on the things you desire. The best thing these affirmative prayers will do for you is to eliminate the negative mental and emotional files that may have you stuck in the rut of believing that where you are is as good as it gets.

A word of caution: do not make your prayer practice more difficult than it needs to be in order to be effective. While there is no right or wrong way to pray, it is still a very sacred and powerful process. What makes your prayers sacred is your intention. In your GOI work, you are being asked to pray immediately upon rising. You may choose to wash your face first, or not. You may want to go to a sacred location, but doing so is not absolutely necessary. You may consider your position, location, or attire, or not.

What I do is this: the moment my eyes open, whether naturally or in response to the alarm, I roll onto my back and take a few deep breaths. I focus my mind and heart on gratitude for a new day, and I recite my prayer—first mentally and then aloud. Then I get out of bed, address all of my personal needs, including washing my face and brushing my teeth, and go to my sacred prayer place to begin my daily prayer practice. Some days I sit in a chair. On other days, I stand. I pray in the same place every day because I have programmed my mind to know that what I do in this place is sacred. You can create your own sacred space, or not. The key here is consistency. Whatever you choose to do and however you choose to do it, do it that way for a period of time before you add or subtract anything.

Your awareness of and ability to align with your Source is just one of the many benefits of a conscious, committed prayer practice. Prayer as a spiritual discipline is a process and practice of establishing communion with the Divine, the Source, the Creator. Whether you identify that essence as God, Jesus, Higher Mind, Love, or by some other name doesn't matter. Your commitment to a consistent connection and awareness of the presence of the Divine in your life will result in a greater sense of peace and connection that supports all that you do in every aspect of your life.

II. Thought Therapy Affirmation: Say It Like You Mean It!

Developing a positive and productive mind-set is the most powerful way to overcome and eliminate dominant negative thought patterns. By uprooting negative thoughts and beliefs and replacing them with positive affirmative thoughts, achieving whatever you desire will be possible. Professionals and businesspeople are now being taught how to use affirmations and other subliminal techniques to gain a competitive edge in the marketplace. This same process put to use in your personal life can transform your thought patterns and emotional energy to produce success and fulfillment.

Affirmations are a method of preparing your mind for success; an unprepared mind cannot entertain, experience, or receive success. An affirmation is a statement you make to impress a desired idea onto your consciousness and within the energy of your environment. It is a *suggestion* that you make to yourself that increases and expands your beliefs and expectations. A suggestion is an idea or plan generally proposed by another person to gain your acceptance and supportive action. Commercial ads are a form of suggestion. Think of an affirmation as an ad for a desired experience that you run in your brain. In this way, an affirmation becomes more than positive self-talk. It becomes a powerful declaration that inspires or motivates acceptance and action.

Using affirmations to impress an idea on your consciousness is the way you build mental or emotional stamina and strength. Like any other workout practice, you must use affirmations consistently in order to reap their benefits. The affirmations presented here are offered to support you throughout your daily work of eliminating dominant negative thought patterns.

Since an affirmation is a declaration—a formal or explicit statement or announcement—please be mindful that when you declare yourself to be something or want something, everything unlike it will show up in your life. Each day that you commit to this practice, everything unlike what you declare will challenge you. People will challenge you, situations and circumstances will challenge you, and for that reason, you must challenge yourself. Remember to use your affirmation when you are being challenged and you begin to believe that the prayers and affirmations are not working.

While you are asked to repeat a specific affirmation five times each day, you may find it helpful to repeat an affirmation to yourself every hour on the hour, or to record it and listen to it throughout the day. If toxic feelings or beliefs surface, use the affirmation offered to counteract them. Remember, you'll be challenged, but you don't have to be defeated by dominant negative thoughts.

Rather than offer a lengthy explanation of how and why affirmations work, I'll share with you an affirmation I was taught about the process and power of affirmation:

All thoughts are creative.

When I think positively, I create powerfully.

My thoughts are affirmations that support the creation of the reality I desire.

My affirmations are the words I speak to powerfully infuse my thoughts.

I repeat my affirmations with emotional commitment, intensity, certainty, and faith.

My affirmations consistently support me as I tap into the unlimited power of my subconscious mind.

Every affirmation I speak has a powerful and positive influence on my mind throughout the day.

My affirmations create new habits that will propel me, with grace and ease, toward all that I desire.

I feed faith and strength into every fiber of my being by using my affirmations consistently and with commitment.

I affirm my good, and I see it come to life.

III. Conscious Breath Work

Feelings come and go like clouds in a windy sky.
Conscious breathing is my anchor.

—THICH NHAT HANH

Can you imagine that after all the years you have been alive, inhaling and exhaling, all day every day, there is a chance that you don't know *how to breathe*? For many of us, breathing is not something we think about, we simply do it; as a result, some of us have very poor breathing habits. While breathing is essential to life, it is rarely considered a necessary part of attracting the good things we desire in life. Poor breathing habits are very common; few of us understand that by practicing conscious breathing we can improve our sleep patterns, reduce stress, boost our overall health, and enhance our capacity to succeed in every area of life. Through conscious breath work and awareness of our breathing patterns, we can increase mental sharpness; generate greater energy levels; and better coordinate our physical, mental, emotional, and spiritual actions. By consciously controlling our breathing patterns, which is common in certain meditative and yogic practices, we can also reverse negative thought patterns.

Our poor breathing habits deprive our bodies of life-sustaining oxygen, which in turn impairs our ability to burn fat, produce energy, think a thought, move a muscle, digest food, or fight bacteria. When we breathe unconsciously, we breathe fast or shallow, which allows the breath to circulate only from the head to the chest rather than throughout the entire body. We also hold our breath or keep our mouths open when we concentrate. These poor breathing habits can be improved, thereby increasing the flow of oxygen throughout our mind and body. When we breathe consciously, we exert control over the inhalation and exhalation of the breath, which means we have a full-body experience of receiving and releasing oxygen.

Correct and conscious breathing is one of the best and easiest ways of building a healthy mind and body. When we breathe consciously, we invoke a relaxation response that is healing, energizing, and cleansing. The correct way to breathe is when the stomach or diaphragm extends or pushes out with the inhale and collapses with the exhale. Most of us breathe in reverse. We suck the stomach in when we inhale and have no clue what happens when we exhale. By breathing consciously, we release stress as well as all of the mental and physical issues associated with the experience of being stressed. Conscious breath work is powerful because it oxygenates the brain and body cells, allowing us to function in a clearer mental and emotional state. It increases circulation to the lymph glands, removing toxins and debris and thereby releasing negative energy.

The following conscious breath work techniques are offered to support you in the work we will do to release dominant negative thought patterns. You are encouraged to choose one and practice it each day before or after your affirmative prayer in the morning and evening. Of course, I encourage you to practice consciously breathing throughout the day, too!

Technique 1: To Balance the Brain

+ Sit cross-legged on the floor or in a chair with your spine erect.

+ Close your eyes.

+ Apply gentle pressure with your thumb to close your right nostril.

+ Inhale deeply through your left nostril to the count of 6.

+ Pause for a count of 2.

+ Remove your thumb, apply gentle pressure with your forefinger to close your left nostril, and exhale completely through your right nostril for a count of 6.

+ Repeat this process 10 to 15 times.

Technique 2: To Establish a Sense of Calm

+ Close your eyes if you can.

+ Inhale through your nose evenly and deeply for a count of 8.

+ Pause for a count of 3.

+ Exhale completely through your nose for a count of 8.

+ Pause for a count of 3.

+ Repeat this process 10 to 15 times.

Technique 3: To Clear and Energize the Entire Body

+ Begin by finding a comfortable position, whether sitting or lying down. (Sitting on the floor with your legs crossed is a good position to try.)

+ Set the intention that you will not fall asleep—that you will stay awake, aware, and alert.

+ Close your eyelids, or focus your gaze on one spot on the wall.

+ Take a long, deep inhale and, with the exhale, begin to relax.

+ Allow a feeling of relaxation to fill your entire body.

+ With every inhale, relax.

+ With every exhale, allow your body to relax even more.

+ Roll your shoulders slowly forward and then slowly backward.

+ Slowly and gently, lower your left ear toward your left shoulder.

+ Then, slowly and gently, lower your right ear toward your right shoulder.

+ Remain focused on inhaling and exhaling as you continue to relax.

+ With every inhale, think "re."

+ With every exhale, think "lax."

+ Repeat this process for a few seconds.

+ Your body will continue to relax as you breathe deeper and deeper.

+ Observe your breathing.

+ Notice how your breath flows in and out.

+ Make no effort to change your breathing in any way, simply notice how your body breathes.

+ Your body knows how much air it needs.

+ If your attention wanders, as it will, bring your focus back again to your breathing, thinking "re" with every inhale and "lax" with every exhale.

+ Notice any stray thoughts, but don't dwell on them.

+ Simply let the thoughts pass.

+ Notice how your breath continues to flow in, deeply and calmly, then flow out, deeply and calmly.

+ Notice the stages of a complete breath: the inhale, the pause that follows, and the exhale.

+ Notice the slight breaks between each breath.

+ Feel the air entering through your nose.

+ Feel the exhale as it passes across your upper lip.

+ If thoughts intrude, allow them to pass and then return your attention to your breathing.

+ Remain aware of your inhale and your exhale.

+ Imagine each breath as it enters, filling your body gently. Feel your chest and stomach gently rise with your inhale.

+ Next imagine each breath as it exits, leaving your body slowly. Feel your chest and stomach gently fall with your exhale.

✦ Now as you inhale, count silently—one, two, three . . .

✦ Pause, gently holding the breath as you count—one, two, three.

✦ As you exhale, count silently—one, two, three.

✦ Again, as you inhale, count silently—one, two, three.

✦ Pause, gently holding the breath—one, two, three.

✦ As you exhale, count silently—one, two, three.

✦ Become aware as you breathe in and out.

✦ Notice now how your body feels.

✦ Notice how calm and gentle your breathing is—does your body feel relaxed?

✦ Breathe in and out.

✦ Now it's time to gently reawaken your body and mind.

✦ With your eyes still closed, notice the sounds around you.

✦ Feel the floor beneath you.

✦ Feel the fabric of your clothes against your skin.

✦ Gently wiggle your fingers and toes.

+ Shrug your shoulders up and let them fall back gently.

+ Now give your body a big stretch.

+ And when you are ready, open your eyes.

You can now resume your normal activity or begin your prayer work.

IV. Thymus Thump

As human beings, we are not "one size fits all." This means that if 10 individuals have the same experience, each one will have a different response to what he or she has seen, heard, or felt. While it's true that we all respond differently to what we experience, we do share a commonality: whatever we experience in life, we experience on all levels of being—mental, emotional, physical, and spiritual. This commonality is what gives rise to the power and effectiveness of EFT (Emotional Freedom Techniques) energy therapy, the gentle art of clearing cellular memory through the human energy field. It works on the concept of the interconnection between the physical, emotional, mental, and spiritual realms of our lives.

Renowned wise woman Christiane Northrup, M.D., author of *Women's Bodies, Women's Health*, has taught us: "*Our emotions and thoughts are always accompanied by biochemical reactions in our bodies. Energy fields interact within an*

individual person, interact between one person and another, and between one person and the world in general. When we begin to appreciate ourselves as fields of energy with the ability to affect the quality of our own experience, we will be getting in touch with our innate ability to heal ourselves and create health every day of our lives, at all levels of our experience."
—CHRISTIANE NORTHRUP, MD

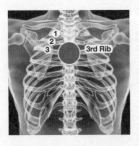

The thymus gland is the primary gland that controls and impacts the body's immune system. The overall function of the immune system is to prevent or limit infection. When the immune system is imbalanced or compromised, the body is prone to infection and disease. This is one reason why people who experience extreme stress are subject to more colds and other viruses. The thymus gland is located in the emotional energy center of the body—behind the sternum, or breastbone—near the heart. In fact, it has been referred to as the "heart's protector." The thymus gland is energetically responsible for regulating the flow of energy throughout the entire body; it's affected most by emotions related to feeling unsafe, attacked, and unprotected—those emotions that accompany most dominant negative thought patterns. Because the thymus is so powerful and connected to the rest of the body's energy system, almost any emotional or energetic blockage or imbalance can be affected by working with the thymus gland. The thymus thump is a method of gently tapping on the thymus gland to create vibrations that stimulate energy within the body.

For the purpose of the work we will be doing, we can use the thymus thump when reciting our prayers and affirmations. Think of it as a sort of spiritual pounding of the chest in the same way a gorilla might pound its chest before entering a battle, or in the same the way an individual may clutch her chest in the midst of a stressful event. In these situations, both the gorilla and the individual are attempting to stimulate the thymus gland and regulate the immune system.

Now it's your turn. Are you ready to clear some stuck energy?

To begin, take a couple of deep, relaxing breaths. Using your fingertips or the side of your fist, tap up and down about 2 to 3 inches along your sternum, between and above your breasts or pecs. (Although the thymus is located behind the third rib, any vibrations along the length of the upper sternum will stimulate it.) Continue to do this for 15 to 20 seconds while taking regular, slow breaths. After thumping on the thymus for the recommended period of time, read through the affirmative prayer you're working with. Once you have read your prayer, again thump your thymus and repeat your affirmation.

V. Thought Therapy Eye Movements

When I shared with those closest to me why I was ending a 14-year relationship, they stared at me as if I had sprouted horns atop my head. I told them, "His eyes no longer light up when I walk into the room." What??? It's often said that "the eyes are the mirror to the soul." I believe you can tell the condition of a person's heart by simply looking into his or her eyes. A mother, for example, can tell when her children are frightened or when they are being less than truthful by looking in their eyes.

Being in a relationship with someone is an important aspect of life. We want to share all of who we are, and we want to know that who we are matters to our beloved. I don't choose to be "just another" person in the life of my beloved. I want to feel and be connected at the soul level. That feeling will be reflected by how he looks at me, what he sees for me, and how I feel when I look at him. Fourteen years is a long time, and during that time, things can become dull, worn out, and taken for granted. My partner was and is a beautiful man, but when I looked into his eyes, it was clear to me that the thrill was gone . . . and so was he. He didn't agree and was willing to convince me otherwise. But I have learned over the years never to allow what someone else says and does to determine how and what I feel.

If there are issues in the soul that the eyes can reveal, this must also mean that the eyes can play an important role in clearing those issues. "Soul," as it is used here, refers to the deepest level of our being. The soul, the core, the essence, the spiritual part of a human being is adversely affected by the dominant negative thought patterns we hold. As we've discussed, there's a file in our brain for every hurt, disappointment, upset, and trauma we've lived through. When a file is opened and a memory surfaces, those deep imprints on our soul are revealed by a dimming of the light in our eyes.

At the physical level, light rays enter the eyes by passing through the cornea, the pupil, and the lens, and then striking the light-sensitive nerve cells (rods and cones) in the retina. Internal and external mental processing begins in the retina when light energy produces chemical changes in the retina's light-sensitive cells. These cells, in turn, produce electrical activity in the brain. Nerve fibers from these cells join at the back of the eye to form the optic nerve. Electrical impulses are communicated to the visual cortex of the brain by way of the optic nerve. The visual cortex makes sense of the electrical impulses and either files the information for future reference or sends a message to a motor area of the body to take some action. When we see or experience something unpleasant or traumatic, the eyes play an important part in what gets communicated to the brain. If we reverse the process, we can communicate with the brain by using the eyes to stimulate a chemical reaction.

Eye movement techniques such as EMDR (eye movement desensitization and reprocessing) have been used quite successfully in helping people who suffer from trauma, anxiety, panic, disturbing memories, post-traumatic stress, and many other emotional problems. EFT (Emotional Freedom Techniques) or "tapping," as it's commonly called, also uses brain-eye movements called the Gamut Procedure to support the reprogramming of the brain when new thoughts and ideas are introduced. In both instances, eye movements are used to eliminate stress surrounding a difficult or traumatic event and to release the corresponding energy held by the brain. In the GOI process, we'll use thought therapy eye movements to stimulate and coordinate the hemispheres of the brain so that your mind will become receptive to the new ideas presented in the affirmative prayers and daily affirmations I offer later in this book.

In order to coordinate the hemispheres of the brain to receive and process this new material, I suggest that you complete one cycle of eye movements before your morning and evening prayer, and again before you repeat your affirmations throughout the day. The thought therapy eye movements are simple and should take you about 10 seconds to complete.

With your eyes open and while holding your head steady, complete the following:

✦ Focus your eyes on a spot on the wall or on a point directly in front of you.

CENTER FOCUS

✦ Stretch your eyes as far up as possible, as if you're trying to see the top of your head;

UP

then bring your eyes back to the focus point.

CENTER FOCUS

✦ Stretch your eyes as far down as possible, as if you're trying to see your feet;

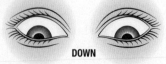

DOWN

then bring your eyes back to the focus point.

CENTER FOCUS

✦ Stretch your eyes up to the right,

RIGHT UPPER

to the center right,

RIGHT CENTER

and far down to the right;

RIGHT LOWER

then bring your eyes back to the focus point.

CENTER FOCUS

✦ Stretch your eyes up to the left,

LEFT UPPER

to the center left,

LEFT CENTER

and far down to the left;

LEFT LOWER

then bring your eyes back to the focus point.

CENTER FOCUS

✦ Stretch your eyes as far up as possible;

UP

then bring your eyes back to the focus point.

CENTER FOCUS

✦ Stretch your eyes as far down as possible;

DOWN

then bring your eyes back to the focus point.

CENTER FOCUS

✦ Now close your eyes, and while holding your head steady, repeat the steps once again.

✦ Stretch your eyes as far up as possible;

UP

then back to their starting point.

CENTER FOCUS

✦ Stretch your eyes as far down as possible;

DOWN

then back to their starting point.

CENTER FOCUS

✦ Stretch your eyes up to the right,

RIGHT UPPER

to the center right,

RIGHT CENTER

and far down to the right;

RIGHT LOWER

then back to their starting point.

CENTER FOCUS

✦ Stretch your eyes up to the left,

LEFT UPPER

to the center left,

LEFT CENTER

and far down to the left;

LEFT LOWER

then back to their starting point.

CENTER FOCUS

✦ Stretch your eyes as far up as possible;

UP

then back to their starting point.

CENTER FOCUS

✦ Stretch your eyes as far down as possible;

DOWN

then back to their starting point.

CENTER FOCUS

Now that you've become more familiar with the five tools in your GOI tool kit—thought therapy prayer, thought therapy affirmation, conscious breath work, thymus thump, and thought therapy eye movements—it's time to practice, practice, practice. Get ready to watch your dominant negative thought patterns (DNTPs) transform into positive thought patterns (PTPs), all because of your commitment and willingness to do your work.

CHAPTER 5

THE GET OVER IT! (GOI) PROCESS

*For there is nothing either good or
bad, but thinking makes it so.*

—WILLIAM SHAKESPEARE, HAMLET

*n*o matter how many thousands of thoughts have been on parade in your consciousness today, I recommend that you activate your healing work in an optimal state of mind. It's essential to affirm your divine intention before you start to do your work. The power of focused intention can never be overestimated, so in that spirit, I offer the Universal Clearing Prayer.

UNIVERSAL CLEARING PRAYER

*I now acknowledge, accept, and know that God's Will
and plan for me is perfect joy and peace.*

My joy and peace depend on my doing my part in God's plan.

My part is to unite my will with God's Will.

It is my intention in this moment to align my will with God's Will, by remembering Who walks with me, so that I will enter into the awareness of God's Presence.

My joy and peace depend on my choosing my essential part in God's plan.

For my joy and peace, I give myself permission to know the truth.

I know that truth will correct all errors in my mind.

I ask that the truth of God's Will be revealed to me now.

I ask that the truth of God's plan be revealed to me now.

I ask. I allow. God becomes the truth I seek.

I now share God's Will for my peace and joy.

God's Will for me is activated in my mind and life now!

Amen!

The good news about the Universal Clearing Prayer is that it can be amended to meet any need. This is accomplished by replacing the words "joy" and "peace" wherever they appear with the subject of your need. For example, if you need clarity about a specific situation, simply replace the words "joy" and "peace" with the word "clarity." Thus, the prayer would read as such: I now acknowledge, accept, and know that God's Will and plan for me is perfect clarity about . . . If you need peace in your relationship with someone, the prayer would read in this way: I now acknowledge, accept, and know that God's Will and plan for me is peace between [insert name] and me . . . If you need to reach the point of understanding about something, the prayer would read like this: I now acknowledge, accept, and know that God's Will and plan for me is understanding why.

Here is an example of how I customized the Universal Clearing Prayer for someone who was starting her own coaching practice.

I now acknowledge, accept, and know that God's Will and plan for me is success in my private coaching practice.

My success depends on my doing my part in God's plan.

My part is to unite my will with God's Will.

It is my intention in this moment to align my will with God's Will, by remembering Who walks with me, so that I will enter into the awareness of God's Presence.

The success of my practice depends on my choosing my essential part in God's plan.

For my success I give myself permission to know the truth.

I know that truth will correct all errors in my mind.

I ask that the truth of God's Will be revealed to me now.

I ask that the truth of God's plan be revealed to me now.

I ask. I allow. God becomes the truth I seek.

I now share God's Will for the success of my private coaching practice.

God's Will for my practice and me is activated in my mind and life now!

DISCOVERING YOUR DNTPs—A SHORTCUT

Even some of my most dedicated students have confessed to me that they often lack the time, energy, or willpower to drill all the way down on their most troublesome DNTPs. They want to stay committed to this invaluable self-healing work, but they exclaim, "We need a shortcut!" So if your life isn't putting you nose to nose with your DNTPs—or if you're an expert at keeping your eyes closed—here's a shortcut to help you identify your priority DNTP assignment.

Either photocopy or write out all of the 42 DNTPs listed on page 157, then cut them into small slips of paper. Fold each slip in half and place the 42 DNTPs into a small basket or bowl.

Now, as though you were poised to choose a prize-winning lottery ticket, set your intention, reach into your container, and choose a dominant negative thought pattern. The one you select will be the one you and the Universe have ordered up as your "work," and you'll begin the healing process by using one or more of the tools in your tool kit: thought therapy prayer and affirmation, conscious breath work, thymus thump, and thought therapy eye movements. You'll focus on neutralizing, healing, or eliminating this DNTP daily for 20 minutes. Most DNTPs can be cleared in two to four daily sessions. Are you ready?

Step 1: Identify Your DNTP and Set Your Intention

Whether you've chosen your DNTP after careful reflection or had it hand delivered from the Universe, the GOI process always begins by asking you to select a specific dominant negative thought pattern that you want to eliminate. Forty-two of the most common dominant negative thought patterns are discussed in Chapter 6, including basic DNTP definitions; the "In Other Words" section that reflects DNTP-based feelings and experiences; and the continuous loop of DNTP "Internal Dialogues" that indicate when a pattern is dominating your mind.

Don't be alarmed if you think you have *all* of the patterns listed; most of us have them all to one degree or another. The key is to identify which ones are blocking you from creating desired changes in your life. At some point, you may want to address all 42. That would be a very wise decision.

Say: "Today the dominant negative thought pattern that I intend to heal is _____."

Step 2: Rate Your DNTP Intensity Level

To determine the intensity level for the DNTP you're working on, you'll use a scale of 0 to10: a 0 rating represents neutral feelings and thoughts about an issue that do not trigger an emotional response in your body; a 10 represents a deep desire to hurt someone or something anytime you think about the issue and the experiences attached to it. This rating will be the way you can measure and assess your progress. To rate your DNTP:

+ Take a deep, cleansing breath and allow your body to settle.

+ Silently affirm "re" when you inhale and "lax" when you exhale. Repeat these syllables 3 to 5 times as you breathe deeply in and out, until your body is relaxed.

+ Bring to mind the one-word dominant negative thought pattern you're working with (eg., abandonment, fear, or rage).

+ Silently say to yourself: "From 1 to 10, what is the intensity of this energy in my being?" Now listen for and write down the first number that comes to mind. If the number is more than 10, record it as 10. Sit silently for a moment to make sure the number you have received feels right to you.

If you don't hear anything, repeat the breathing exercise. If that still doesn't work, recite the Universal Clearing Prayer to bring your mind and intentions into alignment.

As you do the GOI work, the intention is to decrease the DNTP intensity level until you feel a shift in your mind and the intensity level you experience drops to 0. This shift will also be demonstrated by how you respond to and address both new and familiar situations in your life. Chances are you'll discover some things that once set you off no longer do; other things you never considered possible for yourself will present you with no difficulties. The more consistently you practice the GOI work, the better you will get at it. The better you get at doing the work, the easier it will become to make better choices and decisions every day. This is how you can confirm that old files are being emptied and new files are being created.

Step 3: Thought Therapy Prayer

In Chapter 7, I have included 42 affirmative prayers, one for each dominant negative thought pattern that appears in Chapter 6. Affirmative prayers follow a protocol of acknowledging and affirming what is true in the divine realm. Your soul, a.k.a. your authentic self, knows what is true, whether or not you consciously know it or believe it. Affirmative prayers tap into the divine essence of your being and ignite the truth that is buried beneath all the lures and traps of the ego and your physical senses. The prayers I'm offering to support your healing process are constructed to override, neutralize, and eliminate dominant negative thought patterns by creating new mental and emotional files.

Each time you repeat a prayer silently, and each time you earnestly speak it out loud, the affirmation you're working with will create, then deepen, a new tread in your subconscious mind. Permit yourself to believe those words as you repeat them to yourself or speak them aloud. (Also feel free to change the salutation, greeting, and name used for God to whatever feels appropriate for you.) There is no "right way" to pray, and while the prayers I offer may not fit into a traditional religion's perspective of our relationship with prayer, remember that every thought carries energy. Affirmative prayers can and do create new thought patterns that bring about very powerful and productive energies.

You should read and speak the affirmative prayer twice a day: once as soon as you wake up and again just before you retire. Doing your morning and evening prayers as the first and last acts of your day is important. In this way, you are programming your mind before you begin your day and before you end your day, separate from all the various interruptions and distractions that plague you throughout the day.

Step 4: Thought Therapy Affirmations

After your affirmative prayer work, you should repeat the corresponding affirmation that I've provided to support your prayer. As with the prayer work, use your affirmation both silently and out loud. You will begin working with your affirmation right after you offer your morning prayer, then continue to work with the same affirmation four more times throughout the day: once again after breakfast or with your morning coffee, after lunch, after dinner, and then after your bedtime prayer. This means you'll be repeating the affirmation at least five times each day.

Of course, you're free to practice your affirmation more often, if you like. Consciously scheduling the affirmation with waking up, eating your meals, and going to bed simply means you won't need to think about it and you'll be less likely to forget it. If you're likely to skip or miss a meal, consider setting the alarm on your smartphone or tablet to send you a reminder throughout the day to do your affirmation.

Step 5: Energy-clearing: Conscious Breath Work, Thymus Thump, and Thought Therapy Eye Movements

To support the mental and energetic shift you're creating with the prayers and affirmations, you may also choose to use one or more of these energy-clearing tools. Conscious breath work, thymus thump, thought therapy eye movements, visualization, and, of course, meditation are all accepted practices for doing deep transformational work related to higher consciousness. While prayer and affirmation are primarily concerned with creating shifts in your mind, energy, and environment, these vibrational tools help unlock and move the energy within the physical body. By engaging in these activities at the mental, emotional, and physical levels, you will have a full body-mind-spirit experience.

If you are using one or more of the tools offered, incorporate them into your practice as I recommend below. At a minimum, you should use one of the conscious breath work techniques before your morning and evening prayer. If you are incorporating the thymus thump, include it before you pray and after you recite the affirmation. If you are incorporating the thought therapy eye movements, do one cycle before your morning and evening prayer and one cycle before you repeat your affirmations throughout the day.

Step 6: Re-Rate Your DNTP Intensity Level

As you do your GOI work throughout the day, remember your intention is to decrease the DNTP intensity level until you feel a shift in your mind and the intensity level of your experience drops to 0.

— 0 1 2 3 4 5 6 7 8 9 10 —

Step 7: Thought Therapy Journal Work
(optional but highly recommended)

Complete the thought therapy journal work daily.

The following thought therapy journal work will help you focus on your healing work with laser-like precision. You're not required to use this exact format, nor are you obliged to use a real journal. You may choose to use a word-processing program on your computer, the digital recorder on your smartphone, or a sheet of tablet paper. I vote for whatever helps you zero in on your DNTPs consistently. To do that, I suggest that you copy the thought therapy journal work list to your smartphone, tablet, or thumb drive. That way you'll have them available at home, work, or play—whenever or wherever you get triggered. Such easy access will support you in keeping track of anything that comes up during the day and will also keep you accountable to your healing commitment.

Don't make this process more difficult than it needs to be. Follow the steps: become aware of the dominant negative thought pattern or feeling; *acknowledge* the feelings that get triggered; set an intention to be healed of the trigger; accept the intensity level of the pattern; and act—"do your work" until the DNTP's intensity level is reduced to 0. And always support your daily prayer and affirmation practices with the energy-clearing tools.

THOUGHT THERAPY JOURNAL WORK

1. The situation that and/or the people who triggered me today are:

2. The DNTP "In Other Words" or "Internal Dialogue" that reflect my experience are:

3. The DNTP I intend to heal is:

4. This reminds me of:

5. Morning DNTP intensity level (on a scale of 0 to 10).

   — 0   1   2   3   4   5   6   7   8   9   10 —

6. Reflections on my thought therapy prayer practice:

7. Reflections on my thought therapy affirmation practice:

8. Reflections on my energy-clearing tools experience(s):
   ❏ Conscious Breath Work
   ❏ Thymus Thump
   ❏ Thought Therapy Eye Movements

9. Evening DNTP intensity level (on a scale of 0 to10):

   — 0   1   2   3   4   5   6   7   8   9   10 —

10. What I now realize:

DAILY PRACTICE RECAP

The person who sends out positive thoughts activates the world around him positively and draws back to himself positive results.

—NORMAN VINCENT PEALE

As your coach, I must remind you that although the GOI process is deceptively simple, the depth of commitment required to achieve your DNTP-free goal requires that you enforce a zero-tolerance zone for you own excuses. *This is your work, and now is your time!*

GOI Daily Practice

Step 1: Identify your DNTP and set your intention.

Step 2: Rate your DNTP intensity level.

Step 3: Thought therapy prayer and selected energy-clearing tool(s).

Step 4: Thought therapy affirmation and selected energy-clearing tool(s).

Step 5: Energy-clearing tools: conscious breath work, thymus thump, and thought therapy eye movements.

Step 6: Re-rate your DNTP intensity level.

Step 7: Complete your thought therapy journal work (optional but highly recommended).

Resurfacing DNTPs

Sometimes when you're rating a DNTP intensity level, the number fails to decrease; instead, it increases. Do not be alarmed! If memories or thoughts related to a pattern resurface, that does not mean the pattern wasn't cleared. It could simply signal that you haven't yet gotten over the habit of thinking the thoughts or remembering the experience. Some habits die hard. If this should happen, immediately pause and get an intensity level for the thought or memory that has resurfaced. Then complete one cycle of thought therapy eye movements using the following affirmation:

+ With eyes up: I can release this thought/feeling.

UP

+ With eyes down: I will release this thought/feeling.

DOWN

✦ With eyes up to the right: I am ready to release this
thought/feeling.

RIGHT UPPER

✦ With eyes center to the right: I choose to release this
thought/feeling.

RIGHT CENTER

✦ With eyes down to the right: I am releasing this thought/
feeling now.

RIGHT LOWER

✦ With eyes up: I can release this thought/feeling.

UP

✦ With eyes down: I will release this thought/feeling.

DOWN

✦ With eyes up to the left: I am ready to release this thought/
feeling.

LEFT UPPER

✦ With eyes center to the left: I choose to release this
thought/feeling.

LEFT CENTER

✦ With eyes down to the left: I am releasing this thought/
feeling now.

LEFT LOWER

Again, check the intensity level of the thought or memory that has resurfaced. Don't be surprised if it's 0. If the intensity level *has not* been reduced to 0, you can incorporate releasing it into the DNTP work you're currently doing (even if you've since moved on to a different DNTP). The most effective way to do this is to set an intention to heal and release all patterns that are resurfacing. Alternatively, for a day or so, you can return to reciting and speaking aloud the prayer and affirmation for the DNTP associated with the specific thought or memory that has resurfaced. The good news is, *this doesn't have to be hard, and you cannot fail.* Consistency combined with a clear intention will do the trick.

PART III
READY, SET, GET OVER IT!

CHAPTER 6

42
DOMINANT NEGATIVE
THOUGHT PATTERNS
(DNTPs)

Thoughts are like an open ocean,
they can either move you forward within its waves,
or sink you under deep into its abyss.

—ANTHONY LICCIONE

*I*n Chapter 3, Troubled Minds: A Family History, you had an opportunity to see the high price paid when Grandma Annie, her daughter Rose, and her grandson Allen marinated in their subconscious dominant negative thought patterns. These destructive unconscious patterns were passed on from generation to generation. I hope that the Brown family history has helped to heighten your awareness, acknowledgment, and acceptance of DNTPs in other people's lives. Now it's time to act and turn the spotlight on your life.

Your "mission possible," should you choose to accept it, is to clear out all of the files related to the dominant negative thought patterns that you are holding in your mind. You will know the pattern is active if, when you read the definition of the pattern or the "In Other Words" section, a wave of discordant energy is triggered in your body. You will also know that the pattern is active if you have actually heard yourself speak the words from the "Internal Dialogue" section. I recommend that you work with one DNTP at a time. If you work consistently, you should be able to clear a DNTP within two to four daily sessions.

YOUR GET OVER IT! (GOI) JOURNAL

I encourage you to begin your self-healing mission by giving a special gift to yourself—a Get Over It! journal. Whether your journal is a beautifully designed, spiral-bound book from your favorite gift shop or a brightly colored tablet from your local dollar store, applaud yourself today for taking the first step in a life-changing experience.

To begin your in-depth DNTPs exploration, find a quiet space where no one will disturb you for 30 to 60 minutes. Carefully contemplate each of the 42 DNTPs found in the next section. Resist the urge to rush through the pages that follow. Take your time and record your experience with any DNTPs that create sensations in your physical body—e.g., deeper or more shallow breathing, heat, tingling, pain, or free-floating anxiety. If you feel it in your body, claim it in your journal. Also, be willing to write down any intense or unusual memories, visual images, or dialogue fragments that arise in your mind. After you complete your review, list the four DNTPs that have made the strongest impression on you in your GOI journal.

42 DOMINANT NEGATIVE
THOUGHT PATTERNS (DNTPs)

✦

42 DOMINANT NEGATIVE THOUGHT PATTERNS (DNTPs)

1. Abandonment
2. Anger/Rage
3. Anxiety/Worry/Fear
4. Betrayal
5. Bitterness
6. Blame
7. Criticism
8. Defensiveness
9. Disappointment/ Discouragement
10. Distrust/Doubt
11. Failure/Frustration
12. Fear
13. Grief
14. Guilt
15. Hatred
16. Heartache/Heartbreak
17. Helplessness/Hopelessness
18. Hostility
19. Humiliation
20. Hurt/Woundedness
21. Inadequacy/Incompleteness
22. Indecisiveness
23. Insecurity/Self-Consciousness
24. Jealousy
25. Joylessness/Depression
26. Loneliness/Longing
27. Lost
28. Low Self-Esteem/Inferiority
29. Numbness/Disconnectedness
30. Overwhelm
31. Powerlessness
32. Pride
33. Regret
34. Rejection
35. Resentment
36. Sadness/Sorrow
37. Self-Abuse
38. Shame
39. Stubbornness
40. Unappreciated /Unimportant
41. Unsupported
42. Unworthiness/Worthlessness

1

ABANDONMENT

+ The experience of being deserted, stranded, or cast off

+ Being left behind by conscious choice

+ Being left completely and utterly forsaken

IN OTHER WORDS

Everybody you care about has left or leaves you. People who were responsible for you, or to you, chose to walk away, often with no explanation. Something or someone was more important than you, so you got left behind. Anyone who was supposed to be there for you wasn't there. People you stood with, and for, were not there for you when you needed them. While "abandonment" is about people not being able to be there for you, rejection is an expression of not even being wanted.

INTERNAL DIALOGUE

+ *People are never/No one is ever there for me.*

+ *He/She/They deserted me.*

+ *He/She/They left me when I needed him/her/them the most.*

+ *I got dumped.*

2
ANGER/RAGE

+ Intense emotional state caused by displeasure, unhappiness, or indignation

+ Strong feelings of annoyance or hostility

+ Fury, wrath; physical or verbal manifestation of extreme anger

+ Loss of control in response to heightened sense of being helpless or powerless

IN OTHER WORDS

You feel intense heat in your body; your face gets red, your ears grow hot, and you may swear and/or throw things. You lose total control of your mind and mouth and may strike out as a result. Or, you experience the "quiet storm" of anger, during which you smile at people while at the same time plotting how you're going to get even with them later. When rage kicks in, you act on the violent energy of your thoughts and feelings—you just want to punch something or someone. You do and say things that are harmful to yourself and others. Quite often, you feel you're justified. You want to stop yourself, but you can't.

INTERNAL DIALOGUE

+ *I hate him/her/them/this.*

+ *I want to kill/hurt you/them/myself.*

+ *I don't deserve this!*

+ *Why is this happening to me?*

+ *Why did this happen to me?*

+ *I'm not going to take this lying down.*

3

ANXIETY/WORRY/FEAR

+ Intense psychological and emotional distress aroused by real or imagined threat of hurt, harm, or danger

+ Alarm, apprehension, or panic without a specific focus

+ Dread or anticipation of disaster

+ Complete overwhelm; an inability to face or handle what may be required

IN OTHER WORDS

You are just plain old scared! You feel as if you're about to jump out of your skin, and you're not sure why. You sense, believe, or feel something bad, harmful, or dangerous is about to happen. Your imagination is running wild about what could happen or may happen, even when there's no evidence to support your thoughts and feelings. This sense of being out of control and anticipating harm causes you to procrastinate or hesitate. You stay right where you are because it's familiar and safe. Anxiety and worry often lead to competing or opposing needs, desires, or responsibilities.

INTERNAL DIALOGUE

+ *Did I lock the door?*

+ *Am I about to lose my job?*

+ *Does my partner really love me?*

+ *Did I just say something offensive?*

+ *What if I end up homeless?*

+ *Now everybody thinks I'm incompetent.*

+ *He/she didn't answer my text—is he/she mad at me?*

+ *What if my parents/partner/children die? What will I do?*

+ *He/she didn't answer the phone all day—maybe he/she had a stroke or heart attack?*

4
BETRAYAL

+ Violation of integrity; broken trust or confidence

+ Revelations or disclosures that failed to guard, maintain, or fulfill an agreement

+ Deception, disloyalty, corruption

+ Disappointment of hopes or expectations

IN OTHER WORDS

Someone you trusted and cared about threw you under the bus and then backed up over you. Someone did or said something he/she promised not to do. Someone exposed your weaknesses, shortcomings, or private personal matters to get what he/she needed or wanted or, perhaps, just because he/she could.

INTERNAL DIALOGUE

+ *He/She/They lied to me.*

+ *He/She/They always misrepresent things.*

+ *He/She/They deceived me.*

+ *I trusted them, and they exploited me.*

5

BITTERNESS

+ Harsh, disagreeable, or cynical attitude

+ Anger, resentment, or animosity caused by hurtful experiences

+ Nasty or cruel manner resulting from poor or unjust treatment

+ Aggrieved or begrudging sensibility

IN OTHER WORDS
You see the worst possibility first. You see what's wrong with everyone and everything, and you point it out. Nothing makes you happy or brings you joy, and you make sure that everyone knows about it.

INTERNAL DIALOGUE
+ *You get what you deserve.*
+ *So what . . . I don't care . . .*
+ *I shoot first and ask questions later.*
+ *I don't owe you anything.*
+ *Really? Let's see how long that lasts.*

6
BLAME

+ Finding fault with oneself and others

+ Criticism, condemnation, reproach, reprimand

+ False sense of responsibility for others and their condition

+ Avoidance of responsibility and accountability for self; guilt

+ Claiming powerlessness and helplessness; having a victim consciousness

IN OTHER WORDS

Someone does something harmful or hurtful that necessitates a specific reaction on your part. This allows you to hold others responsible for what you do or fail to do. It's all about what they did. The flip side of holding them responsible is making yourself responsible for others. This includes taking on the responsibility for others or events that may have nothing to do with you. You make yourself the reason something did or did not happen.

INTERNAL DIALOGUE

+ *You're so selfish.*

+ *It's all your fault.*

+ *I told you not to do that.*

+ *This is what always happens when you . . .*

+ *What were you thinking?*

+ *Why do you always do this to me?*

+ *You never listen!*

7

CRITICISM

+ Disapproving critique of personal characteristics and/or faults

+ Adverse or denigrating comments

+ Sophisticated analysis and judgment

+ Finding fault; disparagement, condemnation, attack

IN OTHER WORDS

Nothing you do is ever enough/good enough/right. Someone always has something bad, unkind, or unloving to say about you or what you have done. Your weaknesses and shortcomings always seem to get the most attention from everyone or from a specific someone.

INTERNAL DIALOGUE

+ *He/She/They always have something disapproving to say about me.*

+ *He/She/They are always judging me.*

+ *He/She/They never say anything nice/good about me.*

+ *Nothing I do is ever enough/good enough/right.*

8

DEFENSIVENESS

+ Anticipating and/or resisting attack

+ Being sensitive to the threat of confrontation or injury to your ego

+ Preemptive self-protection; being on guard against real or imagined physical, mental, or emotional threats.

IN OTHER WORDS

You always have to explain or defend what you have done. You feel others are making you wrong. No matter what is offered, how it is offered, or by whom it is offered, you hear the negative that is coming to you and about you; then you have to defend yourself against it.

INTERNAL DIALOGUE

+ *I don't mean any harm but . . .*
+ *I was just trying to . . .*
+ *What I meant to say is . . .*
+ *I knew you were going to say . . .*

9

DISAPPOINTMENT/ DISCOURAGEMENT

+ Sadness or displeasure caused by failed hopes, unrealized expectations, or unmet needs

+ Disillusionment caused by broken agreements

+ Feeling let down; expressing or showing lack of fulfillment

+ Lack of courage, hope, or confidence

+ Feeling disheartened and dispirited in response to loss/ failure

+ Loss of desire to try or attempt something

IN OTHER WORDS

You've received a punch in the gut about something that mattered to you. You feel totally let down and or turned off. You receive far less than you wanted, expected, or anticipated. Nothing you want ever turns out the way you want. People never do what they say they will do for you. You're expected to be okay with less than you want. You feel hopeless and often helpless. Nothing makes sense. You don't have the strength or motivation to try anymore. You anticipate the worst happening.

INTERNAL DIALOGUE

+ *Don't get your hopes up.*

+ *Things never work out for me.*

+ *People will/always will let me down.*

+ *He/She/They let me down again.*

+ *I thought they were different*

+ *It won't work.*

+ *Why bother?*

10
DISTRUST/DOUBT

+ Belief in deception or dishonesty; inability or unwillingness to trust

+ Uncertainty; lacking a definite opinion, conviction, or determination

+ Feeling indecisive or unsure, with or without reason

+ Suspicion, hesitancy, vacillation, wavering

IN OTHER WORDS

You're always looking over your shoulder, waiting for the next disaster to show up. It feels as if people are always lying or withholding information. Your first thought is about all that could go wrong. You always voice your doubts and hesitations, and you require constant reassurance. You have great difficulty in making choices and decisions in anticipation of the worst happening.

INTERNAL DIALOGUE

+ *I don't trust you/him/her/it.*

+ *I can't/don't trust people.*

+ *You can't trust people.*

+ *I don't believe you/him/her/it.*

+ *It will never happen.*

+ *I don't know.*

+ *I'm not sure.*

+ *I'm confused.*

+ *It's not going to work.*

+ *If only I were smarter, richer, more attractive.*

11
FAILURE/FRUSTRATION

+ Falling short of success or achievement in something expected, attempted, or desired

+ Defeat, breakdown, malfunction

+ Being stuck or unable to progress; exasperation

+ Feeling blocked from executing changes or achieving an objective or goal

IN OTHER WORDS

You feel defeated and let down about yourself, within yourself. You believe that your errors and missteps cannot be corrected or recovered. You keep trying and get nowhere. Nothing you do or try to do works out in your favor. You are filled with self-recrimination because of bad choices, decisions, or behaviors. Your best efforts reap very little reward.

INTERNAL DIALOGUE

+ *Look what I've done!*

+ *I can't seem to get it right!*

+ *I never do anything right!*

+ *I can't win for losing!*

+ *Damn it! Not again!*

+ *What now?*

12
FEAR

+ Strong distress aroused by anticipation of impending danger

+ Sense of real or imagined pain, threat of hurt, harm, or vulnerability

+ Dread, panic, terror, alarm

+ Anxiety or apprehension over the outcome of a situation

+ Avoidance or hesitation because of the likelihood of an unwelcome outcome

IN OTHER WORDS

You are freaking out, feeling super-vulnerable, jumping out of your skin. You are increasingly and irrationally worried about getting caught, hurt, or exposed. You believe that bad things happen to good people, and now it is your turn. You think that your time is up and there's nothing that you can do to fix the disaster that's headed your way. Your gut check confirms that something really, really bad is about to happen. You've decided that it's better to be safe than sorry, so you have frozen yourself in place.

INTERNAL DIALOGUE

+ *I don't feel safe.*
+ *I'm terrified of what might happen.*
+ *I can't do it because . . .*
+ *It's too dangerous/risky.*
+ *If I speak up, I'll be punished.*
+ *It's truth and consequences! I can't tell the truth!*

13
GRIEF

+ Intense emotional suffering caused by loss, disaster, misfortune, etc.

+ Acute sorrow, deep sadness, heartache, woe

+ Universal reaction to bereavement

IN OTHER WORDS

All the wind has been sucked out of you. You feel depleted and doomed. You no longer have the desire or strength to keep going. You and/or your life no longer have a sense of meaning and purpose.

INTERNAL DIALOGUE

+ *Nothing matters to me anymore.*

+ *I just can't . . .*

+ *Nothing can make me feel better.*

+ *I just want to die.*

+ *Just leave me alone.*

+ *I'll never feel love/joy/peace again.*

14
GUILT

+ Self-reproach, remorse, culpability

+ Sense of regret, wrongness, or imperfection related to your behavior

+ Feelings of having done wrong or committed an offense

+ Feelings of responsibility for the harmful actions of another (e.g., abuse, parents' divorce, death, etc.)

IN OTHER WORDS

It feels as if everyone knows you have done something wrong. You expect to be accused or punished. You feel like hanging your head and hiding your face. There's a dark cloud looming within you and around you. You're an outcast because of what you've done, and you have no idea how to make up for it. Guilt is generally externally referenced (something you did to someone) and experienced in public.

INTERNAL DIALOGUE

+ *It's all my fault!*

+ *How could I have ever done that?*

+ *Everyone knows how terrible I am.*

+ *They'll never forgive me.*
+ *How could I have let this happen?*
+ *I'm so sorry, but there's nothing I can do.*

15
HATRED

+ Feelings of loathing or contempt; extreme dislike or intense aversion

+ Destructive thoughts directed at someone or something

+ Self-hatred and/or self-loathing that engenders destructive behaviors toward others

IN OTHER WORDS

You think, speak, and behave in a cruel and/or negative manner. Your first thoughts about everything and everyone are laced with vengeance. You look for and gravitate toward speech and behaviors designed to cause mental, emotional, or physical harm or hurt to others and often to yourself.

INTERNAL DIALOGUE

+ *I'll destroy him/her/them.*

+ *They deserve to . . .*

+ *I hope _____ happens.*

+ *They need to get . . .*

+ *I hope they never get/do/have . . .*

+ *I should _____ them.*

16

HEARTACHE/HEARTBREAK

+ Overwhelming sense of grief or disappointment

+ Being burdened with great sorrow

+ Suffering caused by physical or emotional loss

+ Devastation, inconsolableness

+ Depression, melancholy, sadness

IN OTHER WORDS

You feel as if life is no longer worth living. It is a chore for you to get up in the morning. You have lost something or someone you desperately loved, wanted, or believed you needed. You have lost your center, your sense of self, or your meaning in life. Your thoughts are preoccupied with what was or could have been.

INTERNAL DIALOGUE

+ *I'll never feel love/joy/peace again.*

+ *Nothing can make me feel better.*

+ *Just leave me alone.*

+ *I just want to die.*

+ *Anything is/would be better than this.*

17

HELPLESSNESS/HOPELESSNESS

+ Defenseless; inability to support or comfort yourself

+ Victim consciousness; feeling routinely deceived, exploited, or injured

+ Inability to change your condition or circumstances

+ Having no remedy or cure, no prospect of change or improvement

+ Despair; no expectation of a good or positive outcome

IN OTHER WORDS

You feel stuck, trapped, or overwhelmed and cannot find a resolution. You dwell on your weaknesses and limitations—real or imagined. You request or expect others to rescue you, and you feel defeated, abandoned, and/or hurt when they do not or cannot. You have either given up or speak about giving up on yourself, your life, and your dreams. You are void of ambition and desire. You avoid situations and people in fear that you cannot handle life's challenges. You don't expect success or good outcomes, so you've stopped trying. You do only what is required and nothing more.

INTERNAL DIALOGUE

+ *I just can't . . .*
+ *I don't know how to . . .*
+ *I don't know what to do.*
+ *I never seem to be able to . . .*
+ *Can you please _____ for me.*
+ *I need help.*
+ *What's the point?*
+ *It's a waste of time.*
+ *Why bother?*
+ *I will/can never . . .*
+ *There's no use/value/purpose.*

18

HOSTILITY

+ Combative actions; unfriendliness; resentment or opposition

+ Thoughts, speech, and behaviors that incite resistance and conflict

+ Aggression, opposition, antagonism

IN OTHER WORDS

Some call you mean; others say you're angry. Your face is fixed in a perpetual scowl. You're a habitual eye roller. You see and speak to the worst in everyone and about everything. You come across as an uncaring or hate-filled individual who is always ready to do battle.

INTERNAL DIALOGUE

+ *You better not . . .*

+ *I've got something for you.*

+ *What are you looking at?*

+ *Don't even look at me.*

+ *I could/should slap you.*

+ *Let me tell you what I'm going to do*

19
HUMILIATION

+ Intense, painful, public loss of dignity or self-respect

+ Disgrace, public embarrassment, degradation

+ Unexpected or unwarranted shaming

+ Feelings of mortification resulting from choice of response or behavior

IN OTHER WORDS

Someone has called you out, put you down, made you the butt of his/her joke, and it was unexpected, unnecessary, or inappropriate. Who you are, what you did, or what you said has been made public by someone or by something you have said or done. Everything about you and your worthiness has been called into question by something you said or did or by what someone else has said or done.

INTERNAL DIALOGUE

+ *Only bad people do things like this.*
+ *If anyone found out, I'd feel terrible.*
+ *Why did I/didn't I do that?*
+ *I just can't help it . . . It's so embarrassing.*

+ *I don't know why I can't/don't/always . . .*

+ *Why can't/don't I ever . . .*

+ *Why do I always . . .*

20

HURT/WOUNDEDNESS

+ Physical, psychological, or emotional pain, upset, or damage

+ Feelings of having been undermined or obstructed

+ Sustaining injury or harm to reputation

+ Intense or long-standing abuse, trauma, or humiliation resulting from dysfunctional interactions or experiences

+ Mental and emotional experience of suffering an injury or offense

IN OTHER WORDS

Something or someone has caused you harm and left you scarred. Your expectations and/or desires have been destroyed, leaving you in a vulnerable and diminished state. While being "hurt" feels temporary, being "wounded" feels permanent, i.e., to be "broken" beyond repair.

INTERNAL DIALOGUE

+ *He/She/They injured/disrespected/humiliated me.*

+ *I can never trust her/him again.*

+ *I am/feel devastated.*

+ *I will never be the same.*

+ *There's just no fixing this.*

+ *This is just who I am.*

+ *I can't go on.*

+ *I want to be different, but I can't.*

+ *I've been irreparably harmed.*

21

INADEQUACY/INCOMPLETENESS

+ Insufficiency, imperfection, defectiveness

+ Lacking; missing something essential

+ Not meeting all of the necessary or appropriate requirements

+ Unable to deal with a situation or with life

IN OTHER WORDS

You just don't measure up. Comparing yourself to others, you can see what they have or are capable of and what you don't have or aren't capable of. You feel less than others, and you either highlight your shortcomings or shrink back to hide them. In the worst-case scenario, you keep trying to prove to others—and to yourself—how great you are, even when you don't really believe it. Incompleteness is an internalized version of inadequacy.

INTERNAL DIALOGUE

+ *I never measure up.*

+ *I just can't because . . .*

+ *I've never been able to . . .*

+ *Something is wrong with me.*

+ *I better not say . . .*

+ *I just don't have what it takes.*

+ *There's something missing in me.*

+ *Why do I feel so incomplete?*

+ *Without _____ , I'll always be on the outside looking in.*

+ *I need a major life makeover.*

22
INDECISIVENESS

+ Inability or unwillingness to make a decision

+ Wavering back and forth between one choice and another

+ Doubting your ability to make a good decision

+ Fear of the consequences of your choices or of making a mistake

IN OTHER WORDS

You cannot or will not make a choice. You change your mind frequently and often can't figure out why, or you fail to communicate your change of mind. There are too many things to consider, and you are afraid to make a mistake. You send out mixed messages about your hopes, wishes, and desires. Often you go along to get along, to avoid the responsibility of making a clear choice.

INTERNAL DIALOGUE

+ *I'm not sure what to do next.*

+ *Whatever! It doesn't matter.*

+ *I'll do whatever you say.*

+ *Whatever you think/do/say is fine.*

23

INSECURITY/
SELF-CONSCIOUSNESS

+ Lacking confidence in self or abilities

+ Feeling unsafe from danger or ridicule

+ Hypervigilant awareness of self in the presence of others

+ Oversensitivity to what is deemed as lacking in self

IN OTHER WORDS

You do not perceive or recognize your self-value and worth. You constantly compare yourself to others and find yourself lacking. You're oversensitive to what is wrong or missing within you. Your self-worth hinges on physical characteristics and abilities rather than an authentic sense of your value. You'll try something new only if you have constant reassurance and affirmation. You rely on others to affirm you and boost your confidence. You spend more time talking about what you can do instead of actually doing it. You're prone to feelings of jealousy and envy.

INTERNAL DIALOGUE

+ *Am I okay?*

+ *Do I look okay?*

+ *I can't do it like that.*

+ *I'm not like everybody else.*

+ *I wish I was more like her.*

+ *I really envy him.*

24
JEALOUSY

+ Resentment and envy of someone's success, achievements, or advantages

+ Rivalry; anxiety or fear of loss of a significant status, privilege, or connection

+ Possessiveness; fear of abandonment or of not being loved

IN OTHER WORDS

You go into fear and upset when someone does something better than you could do it, or when someone gets something you want before you do. You have a habit of being critical of the success of others, and you constantly compare your accomplishments and acquisitions to those of others, in an attempt to put yourself on top.

INTERNAL DIALOGUE

+ *They don't deserve . . .*

+ *You know how they got . . .*

+ *They can't do _____ better than me.*

+ *I have to do/get _____ before they do.*

+ *I think there's something going on.*

+ *Who keeps texting you?*

+ *Where have you been?*

+ *Is there something you need to tell me?*

25
JOYLESSNESS/DEPRESSION

+ Intense experience of unhappiness and loneliness

+ Despair; inability to give or feel any pleasure or satisfaction

+ Gloom, melancholy, somberness

+ Expecting and anticipating the worst possibility

IN OTHER WORDS

You feel lost, alone, misunderstood, or out of place, with a sense of not belonging anywhere or not having a meaning and purpose in life. There is a weight on your mind and in your spirit that can immobilize your physical body. There is a disconnection between the physical reality and the spiritual truth, which may be linked to past trauma or to present and future fears. From a spiritual perspective (rather than psychological or clinical), depression is the hunger of the soul for light, love, and connection.

INTERNAL DIALOGUE

+ *I'm miserable.*
+ *Nothing good ever happens to me.*
+ *I just feel really bad.*
+ *What's the point?*
+ *I give up!*
+ *I feel like I'm drowning.*
+ *Nothing helps.*
+ *This burden is too heavy—I can't carry it.*
+ *I can't seem to put even one foot in front of the other.*

26
LONELINESS/LONGING

+ On your own; without having anyone or anything; having no one else present

+ Intense sense of disconnection and/or undesirability

+ A strong desire or craving for human connection/ companionship

+ Missing someone or something

+ Wanting and yearning for something you do not have

IN OTHER WORDS

You have no one to talk to, no one to lean on, nowhere to go when things get hard. You feel alone, and you hate it. No one and nothing seems to fill the void you feel within. You feel stranded and unimportant, as if you don't matter to anyone. More often than not, you isolate yourself or withdraw to prove that your experience of being alone is real. As a result of your feelings, it's difficult for you to let others in to support or assist you.

INTERNAL DIALOGUE

+ *Why do I feel so all alone?*

+ *Something's missing.*

+ *It's not safe to let anyone in.*

+ *I'd give anything to have someone in my life.*

+ *No one wants me.*

+ *I just don't matter.*

27
LOST

+ Aimless, having no direction, off course

+ Inability to see/find the correct or acceptable course

+ Sense of emotional instability or disorientation

+ Inability to make rational decisions

+ Bewilderment, excessive preoccupation

IN OTHER WORDS

You have no internal grounding or center. Your sense of self and your sense of confidence are depleted or missing because of past trauma or experience. Your intense experiences of helplessness, hopelessness, and inadequacy are rooted in a lack or loss of self-esteem (how you see and hold yourself within yourself). You feel that you have no purpose and that your life has no value, direction, or meaning.

INTERNAL DIALOGUE

+ *I don't know who I am or what I want.*

+ *I keep trying, and I still get nowhere.*

+ *I'm confused.*

+ *Where am I?*

+ *Am I okay?*

+ *I'm overwhelmed and exhausted.*

28

LOW SELF-ESTEEM/ INFERIORITY

+ Experience of self as innately less than; second-rate

+ Lacking strength of character, self-respect, or self-trust

+ Sense of having no value or meaning, mediocrity, lacking self-importance

IN OTHER WORDS

You have no faith or confidence in your abilities. You have a long-held and deeply rooted belief in your own inadequacy. You feel unheard and unseen for who you are or want to be. You may believe you are being tolerated and pushed aside. You tend to be compliant and go along; when that doesn't work, you can become defensive or defiant. The idea that you are an underling is a learned behavior, stemming from being constantly compared to others.

INTERNAL DIALOGUE

+ *I never measure up.*
+ *I flunked the test again.*
+ *I'm such a loser!*
+ *What do you think?*
+ *Everybody's smarter than me.*
+ *I better not say anything.*

29
NUMBNESS/
DISCONNECTEDNESS

✦ Lacking awareness, empathy, or connection to feeling or emotion

✦ Response to harrowing or recurring emotional damage

✦ Decision to avoid emotional demands or connections

✦ Aftermath of trauma; feeling deadened or without sensation

✦ Possible sign of depression

IN OTHER WORDS
You feel empty, detached, unbothered. Nothing gets to you. People may think you're cold or mean, but the truth is, you don't feel anything. You're starting to wonder if you'll ever feel joy or love again, or even if you'll ever have a good belly laugh again.

INTERNAL DIALOGUE
✦ *I can't feel anything.*
✦ *I feel disconnected from everything.*

+ *I feel dead inside.*
+ *I don't know what or how I feel anymore.*
+ *I feel completely empty, like there's nothing left.*
+ *I'm physically and emotionally drained.*

30
OVERWHELM

+ The feeling of being overpowered by mind or emotion

+ Extreme stress, exhaustion, devastation

+ The feeling of being overcome, excessively burdened, or crushed

IN OTHER WORDS

You feel as if you have surpassed your limits and cannot do or take on anything more. You are trying to convince yourself that you can do what you do not believe is possible, or you feel others are expecting you to do what you do not believe you can do. You have nothing more to give but sense that more is required or demanded.

INTERNAL DIALOGUE

+ *I just can't . . .*

+ *I don't know how to . . .*

+ *I don't know what to do.*

+ *I never seem to be able to . . .*

+ *Can you please _____ for me?*

+ *I need help.*

31
POWERLESSNESS

+ Lacking authority and strength

+ A feeling of defenselessness, impotence, weakness

+ Inability to cope or take effective action

+ Having no ability, capacity, or skill to control people or situations

IN OTHER WORDS

You are a victim of people and circumstances and are unable or unwilling to stand up for yourself. This most intense experience of helplessness is a learned behavior. Somewhere along the path, you have lost confidence in your strength and what you have the right to be, do, or possess in life.

INTERNAL DIALOGUE

+ *There's nothing I can/could do about it.*
+ *They made me . . .*
+ *No one listens to me.*
+ *I don't have any clout.*
+ *Don't look at me.*
+ *I'm not strong enough to . . .*

32
PRIDE

+ Inflated sense of self-importance

+ Excessive need to be noticed, praised, approved of, or acknowledged

+ Deeming oneself as better than, more important than, and/ or superior to others

+ Sense of vanity or haughtiness that requires inappropriate reward or recognition

IN OTHER WORDS

As Grandma would say, you are full of yourself, and you want everyone else to know it. You expect credit and recognition for what you do, even when it's not warranted. You're not shy about letting others know what you have done, what you can do, what you are doing, and why it is more important than they are. You're quick to inform others how and why they are less than you. This behavior often masks deep-seated feelings of inadequacy or inferiority.

INTERNAL DIALOGUE

+ *I don't care what you think.*

+ *You just don't get it!*

+ *The rules don't apply to me.*

+ *I've done nothing to apologize for.*

+ *I wouldn't be caught dead with him/her.*

+ *If I can't go first class, I don't go.*

+ *I'll tell you what's wrong with him/her.*

+ *I told you so!*

33
REGRET

+ Sadness or sorrow because of what is lost, gone, done, or not done

+ Second-guessing of past actions or inactions; remorse

+ Pang of guilt or conscience

+ Disappointment with self

IN OTHER WORDS

This is the epitome of "shoulda, coulda, woulda," anchored by guilt. An attempt to unsee what you saw, unhear what you heard, or undo what you did, believing things "shoulda, coulda, woulda" been otherwise.

INTERNAL DIALOGUE

+ *Why didn't I . . .*
+ *I knew I should have . . .*
+ *If only I/they had . . .*
+ *I feel bad because . . .*
+ *I wish I'd been true to myself.*
+ *I wish I hadn't worked so hard.*

+ *I wish I'd said what I really thought.*
+ *I wish I'd been more courageous.*

34
REJECTION

+ Feeling excluded, disregarded, denied, or refused

+ Sense of being discarded as useless or unimportant, without cause or reason

+ Feeling unwanted, forsaken, cast out

IN OTHER WORDS

Without cause or reason (that you accept or understand), you have not received or experienced the attention, recognition, acceptance, or affection you desire or feel you deserve. You feel unwanted and possibly unloved. While "abandonment" is about not being able to be there for you, rejection is a statement of not wanting you. This internal experience in reaction to an external experience can lead to self-rejection.

INTERNAL DIALOGUE

+ *They didn't/don't want me.*

+ *I wasn't right/good enough.*

+ *I was thrown out.*

+ *I'm useless.*

+ *I'm a failure.*

+ *I'm such a loser.*

+ *They act like I'm invisible.*

+ *I'll never be accepted.*

35

RESENTMENT

+ Intense anger, displeasure, or indignation at someone or something that has caused injury or insult

+ Bitterness for having been treated unfairly

+ Unwillingness to accept or forgive an offense

IN OTHER WORDS

You are prone to displaying ill will, strong hostility, or antagonism toward others in response to having received what you believe was unfair treatment. You are not shy about voicing your antagonistic thoughts or feelings about people and situations.

INTERNAL DIALOGUE

+ *It's so unfair.*
+ *With friends like these, who needs enemies?*
+ *Why does he/she always take credit for things he/she didn't do?*
+ *They're a bunch of frauds.*
+ *I'll never forgive, and I'll never forget.*

36
SADNESS/SORROW

+ Unhappiness, depression, the blues, despondency

+ Mournfulness, agitation, heartbreak

+ Feelings of grief, burden, torment

+ Experience of loss

IN OTHER WORDS

Sadness is an internal experience caused by repetitive trauma. It's based in the expectation of a hurtful, disappointing, or challenging event that results in dashed hopes or dismay.

INTERNAL DIALOGUE

+ *It doesn't matter.*

+ *I don't matter.*

+ *I'm inconsolable.*

+ *My spirit is grief-stricken.*

+ *I'll never get any better.*

+ *I'm heartbroken.*

37
SELF-ABUSE

+ Negative self-talk, self-inflicted psychological assault or battery, self-blame, etc.

+ Mistreatment of the body with addictive substances, lack of sleep, poor nutrition, or excessive work

+ Punishing or taxing yourself excessively due to anger

+ Harsh atonement for real or imagined defects and deficits

+ Self-mutilation or other forms of self-harm

IN OTHER WORDS

You do not like or love yourself because of what you have been taught or told is true about yourself. Self-abuse is a learned behavior rooted in a poor self-image, a distorted sense of self, and a belief in worthlessness. In most instances, self-abuse is a reaction to external abuse and/or neglect.

INTERNAL DIALOGUE

+ *I deserve to be punished.*

+ *I'm worthless.*

+ *I'm disgusting.*

+ *It's all my fault.*

+ *I'm always hard on myself.*

+ *I didn't mean to hurt myself.*

38
SHAME

+ Feelings of embarrassment or humiliation because of your actions, characteristics, or associations

+ Mortification; sense of distress caused by feelings of stupidity or disgrace

+ Sorrow, contrition, regret, embarrassment

+ Sense of wrongness or distress related to your identity

+ Imposed or accepted sense of a diminished self

IN OTHER WORDS

You feel like you want to, or need to, hide. You feel bad about yourself due to guilt over shortcomings, bad behavior, or wrongdoing. You feel discredited because you have failed to meet your own standards of behavior or personhood. While guilt is public and external, shame is private and internal. Shame is the feeling that there's something deeply and profoundly wrong with you. Shame is rooted in the belief that not only have you failed to be or do your best, you have also brought dishonor upon yourself.

INTERNAL DIALOGUE

+ *What did I do now?*

+ *Why is everything my fault?*

+ *It's always my fault.*

+ *I must have done something wrong.*

+ *Only bad people do things like this.*

+ *If anyone found out, I'd feel terrible.*

+ *Why did I/didn't I do that?*

+ *I just can't help it . . . It's so embarrassing.*

+ *I don't know why I can't/don't always . . .*

+ *Why do I always . . .*

39
STUBBORNNESS

+ Headstrong and obstinate reactions to others' views or positions

+ Inability or unwillingness to cooperate with others

+ Resistance to others, closed-mindedness

+ Refusal to yield, show flexibility, or bend

IN OTHER WORDS

You will dig your heels in and hold to your position or opinion no matter what it costs you or others. Your narrow-mindedness and perspective, often grounded in fear and/or the experience of inadequacy, motivates your choices and decisions as a means for keeping yourself safe.

INTERNAL DIALOGUE

+ *I don't want to.*
+ *No, I hate that!*
+ *You're not the boss of me.*
+ *I'm going to do what I want to do anyway.*
+ *You're wrong!*
+ *Nothing you can say will make me change my mind.*
+ *I'm going to do it with or without you.*

40

UNAPPRECIATED/ UNIMPORTANT

+ Being treated with careless indifference or disrespect

+ Not receiving gratitude for something accomplished

+ Lacking importance or significance

+ Feeling dismissed or ignored as inconsequential, negligible, or shallow

IN OTHER WORDS

You feel that after all you have given or done, there's been no recognition or acknowledgment. You feel taken for granted or in some way dishonored. You may diminish, demean, or devalue who you are and what you offer, or you experience these feelings at the hands of others. In some instances, the need for acknowledgment is based on the need for external validation of who you are and what you do. However, it's perfectly acceptable to desire a thank-you for something you've done well.

INTERNAL DIALOGUE

+ *They never say thank you.*

+ *They always expect me to be there for them.*

+ *A thank-you would be nice.*

+ *They always take me for granted.*

+ *I feel used.*

+ *They must think I'm stupid.*

+ *I don't/it doesn't matter.*

+ *What I want doesn't matter.*

41
UNSUPPORTED

+ Lacking structural support, help, or encouragement (whether real or imagined)

+ Not being provided for by another; not being defended when help is needed

+ Feeling the burden is too heavy to bear alone

IN OTHER WORDS

You have no one to talk to, no one to lean on, nowhere to go when things get hard. You feel stranded and often unimportant, as if you don't matter to anyone. Whether real or imagined, feeling that "no one has your back" represents a void created by not knowing or not asking for what you need and want. You expect that others "should know" how to support you when they simply may not know what you need/ want; or you expect others "should know" you need/want support even when you haven't asked for it. (Remember: there's a difference between not getting what you've asked for and not asking for what you need/want.)

INTERNAL DIALOGUE

- *Why doesn't anyone ever help me?*
- *I just can't handle this all by myself.*
- *No one is ever on my side.*
- *I shouldn't have to ask for your help.*
- *You're never on my side.*
- *You always discourage me.*

42

UNWORTHINESS/
WORTHLESSNESS

+ One who has no good qualities or is useless

+ Good for nothing; having no real value

+ Not commendable or credible

+ Deserving of contempt; possessing no redeeming qualities

IN OTHER WORDS

You do not feel entitled to or deserving of goodness or love.
It's challenging for you to recognize, accept, or acknowledge
your own value. It's challenging for you to receive or accept
a compliment or affirmation. You can always find something
wrong about you or your accomplishments when they're
acknowledged. Worthlessness is a heightened, intense, and
more harmful experience and expression of inadequacy and
unworthiness. With worthlessness, you have no redeeming
qualities, which may give rise to a belief that you don't
deserve to live. Unworthiness can lead to or result from
suicidal ideations, eating disorders, and substance abuse.

INTERNAL DIALOGUE

+ *I don't deserve it.*

+ *I can't accept it.*

+ *If you knew the truth about me, you would . . .*

+ *If you knew the truth about me, you wouldn't . . .*

+ *I'm just good for nothing.*

+ *I can't do anything right.*

+ *I can't fix it or change it.*

+ *Why am I even here?*

+ *I'm not worth two cents.*

+ *I'm going to turn out just like . . .*

CHAPTER 7

42
THOUGHT THERAPY
PRAYERS AND
AFFIRMATIONS

*Our thoughts are mainly controlled by our
subconscious, which is largely formed before
the age of 6, and you cannot change the
subconscious mind by just thinking about it.
That's why the power of positive thinking
will not work for most people.
The subconscious mind is like a tape player.
Until you change the tape, it will not change.*

—BRUCE LIPTON

— 1 —

Prayer and Affirmation to Neutralize, Heal, and Eliminate

ABANDONMENT

Dear God:

I acknowledge You, God, as my ever-present Source of life and love.

I acknowledge Your presence within me.

With You and in You, I know I am never alone.

I ask to feel Your love flowing into and through me in this moment.

I ask for and open myself to be healed from all thoughts, feelings, beliefs, and behaviors related to abandonment.

I ask that every memory, fear, and expectation of abandonment be cleansed and released from my mind, my heart, and my soul.

Acknowledging You as my constant friend and companion, I ask that every person whom I believe has ever abandoned me be surrounded and blessed by the pure light of Your presence in my mind.

I ask that any hurt and all wounds caused by the experiences I have named "abandonment" be filled with the presence of Your love so that they will be healed.

Remind me, God, that You love me.

Allow me to remember that You are always with me.

Fill the empty places in my mind and heart with the fullness of Your grace so that I will know how to and when to let go.

I now proclaim my total and complete healing.

I call forth situations and circumstances that allow me to know and feel love.

I am deeply and profoundly grateful for the power and grace of love present within me and for me.

I release the power of these words, knowing that as I let go and let God, it is done.

And so it is!

Amen.

Affirmation:

The love and light of my life has never and will never abandon me. I am filled with and surrounded by the good that is God, always.

— 2 —

Prayer and Affirmation to Neutralize, Heal, and Eliminate

ANGER/RAGE

Dear God:

I acknowledge You as All Powerful.

There is no thought, no force, no adversary, and no condition more powerful than You.

Acknowledging who and what You are, I ask for and open myself to receive a cleansing of my heart today.

I ask for and open myself to receive a clearing of my mind today.

I ask for and open myself to receive the growing of You within me as the fruits of kindness, gentleness, meekness, and love today.

I ask that You remove from me all vestiges of anger and rage, in all of their forms, at their deepest root and cause.

You are the power in my life.

Any power that I have or express comes directly from You.

Because You live within me, any experience or expression of anger dishonors You.

I ask for and open my heart to be healed of anger today.

I ask for and open my mind to be freed from rage today.

I ask for and open myself to receive the growing of You within me as understanding, compassion, and peace today.

I ask that You remove from me all attachments to anger and rage, in all of their forms, at their deepest root and cause.

Thank You, God, for being the peaceful power that works through me.

Thank You, God, for opening my mind to a deeper awareness of You.

Thank You, God, for opening my heart to a greater experience of You.

Thank You, God, for being more powerful than any thoughts of or beliefs about my right to hold on to anger.

Thank You, God, for the way You show up to clear, cleanse, and heal me.

I ask! I allow! God becomes the healing and peace I desire.

I let it be!

And so it is!

Affirmation:

Anger and rage are my enemies. I give myself permission to lovingly release all anger now.

— 3 —

Prayer and Affirmation to Neutralize, Heal, and Eliminate

ANXIETY/WORRY/FEAR

My Lord, My Lord:

I am in distress. I feel anxious and afraid. I am desperately seeking peace.

There is a war within me that only You can resolve.

There is fear in my heart that only You can remove.

There is conflict in my mind that only You can heal.

I ask You, my Lord, to remove the anxious energy in the pit of my stomach.

I ask You, my Lord, to uproot and remove the source of the anxiety and conflict in my heart.

I ask You to fill me with the presence of peace and calm and right thinking now.

Peace in my mind. Peace in my heart. Peace in my soul.

Send Your ministering angels to fill me with peace now.

I surrender my mind to the presence of Your peace.

I surrender my heart to the presence of Your love.

I surrender my life to the wisdom of Your presence.

I surrender all anxiety, conflict, confusion, and fear into Your hands.

I decree and declare that everything I release to You is now replaced with peace.

I am so very grateful for this opportunity to lean on You.

I am so very grateful that Your strength, Your wisdom, Your love, and Your grace are surrounding and infilling me right now.

I claim peace and clarity in my mind now.

I claim peace and calm in my heart now.

I claim my freedom from any and all forms of anxiety, confusion, worry, conflict, and fear.

My mind is free now. My heart is open now. My soul is free now.

I am so very grateful that this prayer has been answered, and that peace now dwells in my soul.

I rest in Thee.

I let it be!

And so it is!

Affirmation:

Boldly, I stand in the peaceful freedom that dissolves all anxiety, confusion, worry, and fear.

— 4 —

Prayer and Affirmation to Neutralize, Heal, and Eliminate

BETRAYAL

Just Now, Dear Lord:

I confess feeling betrayed by people, circumstances, and situations.

I confess that I have betrayed myself at times.

I confess the need to understand certain people and things. I confess the feeling of betrayal when people demonstrate they are not who or what I want or need them to be.

I confess the need to understand why things happen the way they happen.

I confess, dear Lord, that there have been times when I believed that You had betrayed me.

Just now, in this moment and for all time, I surrender every thought, belief, behavior, understanding, learning, or attachment to the experience of betrayal.

I surrender feeling betrayed, being betrayed, and looking for signs or evidence of having been betrayed.

I choose to shift my focus from people and things and direct my focus on who You are within me, who You are to me, and who You are for me.

In Your presence, all betrayal is brought to naught and nothingness.

With Your presence, betrayal has no power in my mind, my heart, or my life.

As the presence of You in human form, betrayal has no power within me or over me.

I choose to focus my attention on Who protects me, Who guides me, and Who loves me.

I now declare that, as I shift my focus, all sorrow and suffering is lifted from my heart.

As I focus my attention on trusting You, I know that everything is in Divine Order.

I know that all seeds and roots of betrayal are eliminated from my life.

Thank You, God, for receiving this prayer.

Thank You for the healing that is now an aspect of every fiber of my being.

Thank You for healing in my life and in all my affairs.

I am grateful for the healing in this moment and all moments to come.

I rest in Thee.

I let it be!

And so it is!

Affirmation:
I now trust who God is within me, who God is to me, and who God is for me, knowing I shall not be betrayed.

— 5 —

Prayer and Affirmation to Neutralize, Heal, and Eliminate

BITTERNESS

Dear God:

Thank You for the sweetness of Your love within me.

It is this sweetness that I now call forth to heal my heart of bitterness.

Thank You for the invitation to come aside and rest in You.

In Your presence, all bitterness dissolves.

I confess there are times when I have allowed bitterness to reign in my heart.

Today, I lay aside all bitterness and all defenses.

You call my name so gently, inviting me to spend time in Your sweet presence.

You invite me to step away from the noise, away from the day, away from my agenda, and away from the internal dialogue and mental chatter that can make me feel bitter, overwhelmed, and frustrated.

You remind me that You long to hear my prayers and that my well-being is important to You.

It is my heartfelt desire to be in the center of Your will.

It is my heartfelt desire to be a demonstration of the sweetness and joy of life.

It is my heartfelt desire for You to be pleased with me and within me.

I come aside with an open heart and willing spirit.

Anoint me afresh! Bless me, God! Remove the stain of bitterness from my heart.

Rain down miracles and drench me in the gentle sweetness of Your presence within me.

I surrender all things that are displeasing to You.

Thank You, God, for the invitation to remember and be with You.

Thank You, God, for this moment in time.

Thank You, God, for Your attention.

Thank You, God, for sweetening my mind and heart with Your Spirit.

I ask! I allow! God becomes!

And so it is!

Amen.

—*Offered by Rev. Manazerine Olujimi Baptiste*

Affirmation:

I surrender all bitterness to accept the presence of God's sweetness and joy in my heart.

— 6 —

Prayer and Affirmation to Neutralize, Heal, and Eliminate

BLAME

Dear God:

I ask for and open myself to receive the presence of Your wisdom.

I ask for and open myself to recognize the truth.

I ask for correction and open myself to be directed.

I ask for and open myself to be healed of all thoughts, feelings, and beliefs that lead to or support the tendency toward or habit of blaming others.

I ask for and open myself to be delivered from whatever it is within me that motivates me to make others responsible for what I do or do not do; what I say or do not say; what I have and do not have.

Help me, God, to see myself and others rightly.

Help me to stand in the fullness of power and purpose that You have given my life.

Help me, God, to know that You are the reason and the cause for every moment of my life.

Help me to recognize that I am learning and growing through every experience.

Lift from my eyes the veil that prevents me from seeing how I contribute to those things I blame others for doing.

Open my ears so that I will hear and recognize any mixed blame messages in my speaking.

Open my heart so that I will accept any correction that You may want me to receive.

I affirm and accept the power of Your presence within me.

I surrender and release anything and everything in my mind or heart that motivates me to look outward before I turn within.

I turn within to You right now as my Source and my Creator.

I turn within to the presence of Your love and light.

I accept total and complete responsibility for every aspect of my mind, life, and being.

I now choose to bring my mind, heart, and life into perfect alignment with Your will.

I surrender all blame and finger-pointing.

I claim total, complete, and perfect healing in my mind and heart.

I rest in Thee.

I let it be!

And so it is!

Affirmation:

There is no one to blame. Standing prayerfully and powerfully, I accept full responsibility for every aspect of my life.

— 7 —

Prayer and Affirmation to Neutralize, Heal, and Eliminate

CRITICISM

Merciful, Beautiful, and Beloved All-Mighty God:

I just want to take a minute to thank You for all You are doing in my life.

I thank You, God, for the love of family and friends, and for Your loving angels, who bless my path and offer support.

I thank You, God, for waking me up this morning and blessing me with energy and strength to move about my day in the spirit of love, hope, faith, and service.

I thank You, God, for the encouragement that always supports me in moving forward.

I thank You for shining a light on my path and providing me with the courage to walk through challenging times in life without giving up or giving in.

I thank You, God, for teaching me how to be patient with myself and how best to take care of me.

I thank You, God, for teaching me how to be patient with others when I don't agree with or accept their behavior.

I thank You for teaching me the power of yes.

I thank You for teaching me the power of no.

I thank You for teaching me the power of choice.

I thank You for teaching me how to use my voice powerfully and authentically.

I thank You for teaching me the difference between harmful criticism and useful feedback.

I thank You for giving me clarity when I cannot distinguish the difference between confusion and fear.

I thank You for giving me a solid heart and a steady spirit that allow me to face anything that comes my way.

I thank You for all I am on this journey of life.

I am grateful for the lessons and the blessings that await me in each moment.

Teach me, God, how to recognize my lessons and accept my blessings.

Teach me how to be a blessing to others.

I am so grateful!

Amen.

Affirmation:

Today I filter everything I see and hear through the loving presence of God. God helps me to see and to hear all things rightly.

—Offered by Rev. Danielle Hatchell

— 8 —

Prayer and Affirmation to Neutralize, Heal, and Eliminate

DEFENSIVENESS

Most High, Wise, and Holy Source of My Life:

In You, dear God, I live, move, and have my being.

In You I find wisdom.

With You I have power.

Right now, I confess that I have not always made myself available to hear Your voice.

I confess that I have not always made myself available and willing to obey Your word.

I confess that I have not always been willing to reach out for support when I was consumed with anger or doubt or fear.

I confess that I see and feel that others are against me, and that breaks my heart.

I confess that I live on the defense, waiting for the next attack.

I confess that I sometimes attack first.

I am so grateful there is such a thing as grace.

Today, I ask to be healed by Your grace.

I lift my heart and mind in gratitude, knowing You do not hold my missteps against me.

Today, I ask to be surrounded and filled with Your mercy.

I am grateful that I can make a new choice.

In this moment, I choose to surrender my mental and verbal weapons.

I choose to lay down all defenses and defense mechanisms.

In this moment, I choose to release myself from all fear of attack and from all attacking thoughts.

In this moment, I choose to be available to You and obedient to Your will.

In this moment, I choose to hear Your voice and listen for Your instructions.

I am grateful for the opportunity to self-correct.

I am grateful for the opportunity to get out of Your way and to allow Your light and love to shine in, through, and as me.

I am grateful for the opportunity to allow Your power to be revealed in and through me.

I am grateful for Your presence, which protects me from all harm.

Amen and Amen.

Affirmation:
In God, I live. To God, I listen. With God, I need no defenses.

— 9 —

Prayer and Affirmation to Neutralize, Heal, and Eliminate

DISAPPOINTMENT/ DISCOURAGEMENT

Precious Lord of the Universe:

Your Love is lifting me from my yesterday into my right now.

Your Love is lifting me from fear and doubt into a blessed assurance.

Your Love is lifting me from guilt and shame into forgiveness and compassion.

Your Love is lifting me from heartbreak into profound love and laughter.

Your Love is lifting me from sorrow and pain into joy and happiness.

Your Love is lifting me from lack and limitation into abundant thinking and prosperous opportunities.

Your Love is lifting me from self-imposed limitations into infinite possibilities.

Your Love is lifting me from complaining and resistance into gratitude and surrender.

Your Love is lifting me from overwhelm into grace.

Your Love is lifting me out of my story into my power.

Your Love is lifting me out of the shadows into the light of my greatness.

Your Love is lifting me out of inauthenticity into truth and alignment.

Your Love is lifting me out of the self I've created into my divine and authentic identity.

Your Love is lifting me out of victimhood into self-value and a renewed sense of worth.

Your Love has already lifted me out of the valley of human despair onto the mountaintop of Your love.

Your love is with me and in me as it continues to lift me higher.

For this and for much more, I am so grateful.

Thank You!

Amen and Ache.

—Offered by Rev. Manazerine Olujimi Baptiste

Affirmation:

I shall not be disappointed! I am lifted above all self-imposed limitations by the love of God, which fills my heart.

— 10 —

Prayer and Affirmation to
Neutralize, Heal, and Eliminate
DISTRUST/DOUBT

Precious Lord:

Lead me beside the still waters of Your love.

Let my soul be anchored in trust.

Restore in my soul a sense of faith.

Let my soul be anchored in trust.

Lead me onto a path of right knowing and right action.

Let my soul be anchored in trust.

Lift the veil of fear from my mind and my eyes.

Let my soul be anchored in trust.

Illuminate me so that I will know the truth.

Let my soul be anchored in trust.

Strengthen me in the deepest places of my mind so that I will feel secure.

Let my soul be anchored in trust.

Open my heart so that I will accept whatever comes as a gift from You.

Let my soul be anchored in trust.

Remind me that I can trust You.

Let my soul be anchored in trust.
Teach me to trust myself.
Let my soul be anchored in trust.
Give me the wisdom and courage to trust others.
Let my soul be anchored in trust.
Protect me from all perceived hurt, harm, and danger.
Let my soul be anchored in trust.
Settle my mind, heart, and spirit so that I will know and feel Your presence.
Let my soul be anchored in trust.
In Thee, precious Lord, I place my trust.
I feel that You are with me.
I know that You hear me.
I trust that You are guiding me.
I surrender all fear and hesitation.
I rest in Thee.
Let my soul be anchored in trust.
I let it be!
And so it is!

Affirmation:
My soul is filled with and fueled by my perfect trust in God. All is well with me.

— 11 —

Prayer and Affirmation to Neutralize, Heal, and Eliminate

FAILURE/FRUSTRATION

Precious Lord, My Loving Father:

I now ask for and open my mind and heart to receive an outpouring of Your divine light, Your radiant love, and Your perfect healing.

Open me where I have been closed.

Soften me where I have been resistant.

Strengthen me where I have been defiant. Guide me into the places where I have been afraid to go.

I am choosing to see. I am choosing to hear. I am choosing to know.

I am choosing to be all that You have created me to be, to do, and to have.

I am choosing to move in the direction You will for me.

Help me to realize, recognize, accept, and understand that all things are lessons You would have me learn.

Help me to realize that in You there is no failure.

Teach me how to recognize how I do, what I do, so that I will learn how to be and do better.

Lead me into the acceptance of Your will and the understanding that Your will is always for my higher good.

Thank You for reminding me that it's not too late.

No matter what is done or not done, it's not too late.

No matter what I have or don't have, it's not too late.

No matter where I am or where I am not, it's not too late.

Today, I ask that You erase all mistaken judgments of myself and of You.

Prepare me for a new beginning because I now know, accept, and understand that it's not too late.

Holy Spirit, come!

Thank You!

And so it is!

Affirmation:

God's will for me is unfolding in the right time, in the right way. It's never too late.

— 12 —

Prayer and Affirmation to Neutralize, Heal, and Eliminate

FEAR

Dear God:

Today, I ask that You remind me to remember that I need but call and You will answer.

When my mind is racing frantically, I need but call and You will answer.

When my heart and spirit are gripped with fear, I need but call and You will answer.

When I am faced with difficult decisions and filled with doubt, I need but call and You will answer.

When the pressures and responsibilities of life threaten to overwhelm and overtake me, I need but call and You will answer.

When I feel alone and abandoned, I need but call and You will answer.

When my best efforts do not turn out as I expected, I need but call and You will answer.

When I remember the mistakes and missteps of my past, I need but call and You will answer.

When I am tempted to do what is easy, knowing it's not best for me, I need but call and You will answer.

When I feel obligated to go along just to get along, I need but call and You will answer.

When there's a truth in my heart that I am afraid to speak, I need but call and You will answer.

When my next steps are unclear and I'm afraid to move, I need but call and You will answer.

When I have reached the boundaries of my human strength, I need but call and You will answer.

For every doubt, I need but call and You will answer.

With every question, I need but call and You will answer.

When I find myself in the grips of fear, I need but call and You will answer.

Thank You, God, for loving me enough to answer my call, always.

Today, I ask that You remind me to remember that any time I call, You will answer.

I rest in Thee.

I believe! I know! God responds!

And so it is!

Affirmation:
There is nothing to fear! God's strength and power are on my side. I need but call and He will answer.

— 13 —

Prayer and Affirmation to Neutralize, Heal, and Eliminate

GRIEF

Blessed and Divine Holy Spirit:

Today, in this moment, I ask to be freed from the weight of grief.

Today, in this moment, I ask to be lifted from the pit of sorrow.

Today, in this moment, I surrender all attachment to loss.

I confess to feeling heavy in my soul.

I confess to having darkness in my mind.

I confess to holding sorrow in my heart.

I confess that I don't understand what has happened and why it has happened.

I confess that I am holding thoughts and beliefs that block, deny, and obstruct my experience and expression of joy.

Today, in this moment, knowing that You will respond, I ask for and open myself to receive the fullness of Your healing presence.

Today, I ask for, accept, and allow myself to receive Your love.

Today, I ask for, accept, and allow myself to receive the presence of Your light.

Today, I accept Your will, and I surrender all questions about and resistance to why or how things happen.

I ask for, accept, and allow myself to receive all the goodness that You have prepared for me.

I ask for, accept, and allow Your love and light to flow to me and through me, ending all sorrow, suffering, and grief.

I declare that all is well within me and for me.

Faithfully, I come into Your presence, knowing peace is my only option.

For this I am so grateful.

And so it is!

Affirmation:
I accept the peaceful, loving comfort of the Holy Spirit. I surrender all grief!

— 14 —

Prayer and Affirmation to Neutralize, Heal, and Eliminate

GUILT

Most Divine Holy Spirit:

I acknowledge and confess my limits and frailties as a human being.

I acknowledge and confess the errors of my thinking, the fickleness of my heart, and the unloving tendencies demonstrated by my behaviors.

I acknowledge and confess that my spirit is always willing and that my humanness is often weak.

I acknowledge and confess that my thinking and behavior has resulted in overwhelming feelings of guilt and remorse.

Today, I ask that You lift the veil of all false images and pretenses that have created or resulted in the presence of guilt in my consciousness.

Today, I ask for and open myself to receive and experience Your forgiveness.

Today, I forgive myself for my human shortcomings and shortsightedness.

Today, I forgive myself for lack of and lapses of integrity, honor, respect, and love for myself and all others.

I forgive myself for forgetting that God loves me.

I forgive myself for the judgments I have held about and against myself and others.

I forgive myself for all judgments I projected onto others and into the world.

I forgive myself for allowing myself to believe that what I do and who I am do not matter.

I forgive myself for the ways I have not honored God's presence within me and myself as the presence of God.

I forgive myself for every thought and belief that has blocked my ability to demonstrate God's presence and perfection as the truth of who I am.

I now open my mind, my heart, and my soul to be cleansed and healed with the freedom of God's love.

I now decree and declare that I am freed from the chains and ravages of guilt.

Guide me, Holy Spirit, so that I will make amends where I can.

Heal me, Holy Spirit, so that I am totally and completely freed from the errors and mistakes of the past.

I rest in Thee.

I let it be!

And so it is!

Affirmation:
I am freed from all guilt. I am free to choose. I am free to be a demonstration of God's goodness.

— 15 —

Prayer and Affirmation to Neutralize, Heal, and Eliminate

HATRED

Precious Lord of My Life:

Help me now! Heal me now! Free me now!

I have been overtaken by the darkness of hatred.

My thoughts are filled with anger and vengeance.

My heart is filled with loathing and despair.

I seem to be unable to help myself or change myself.

Somehow, the light of Your presence within me has been dimmed.

Help me now! Heal me now! Free me now!

I desire to feel the presence of love.

I desire to know the peace of love.

I desire to experience and express love toward myself and all others.

I acknowledge that the presence of love is what I need to overcome the darkness of hate.

Help me now! Heal me now! Free me now!

Teach me how to see and know myself beyond the unkind and unloving thoughts I have entertained.

Teach me how to see and know myself beyond the shame, guilt, regret, resentment, or bitterness I may be holding, hiding, denying, or avoiding in the recesses of my heart.

Remind me to remember that Your vision of me and for me is grounded in love and forgiveness.

Help me now! Heal me now! Free me now!

I open my mind and heart to be healed and freed from the darkness of hatred so that I will receive Your love and forgiveness.

I open my mind and heart to be healed and freed from the sting of hatred so that I will remember and live the truth of who I am.

Into Your heart and hands I surrender my mind, my heart, my soul, and my life, knowing that the presence of Your light and love will heal me of all darkness.

I am so grateful for the privilege of life.

I am so grateful for the presence of love.

I am so grateful to know that because I have asked, I am healed and freed from hatred.

I rest in Thee.

I let it be!

And so I am!

Amen and Ache.

Affirmation:

In the presence of divine love and light, I am healed and freed of hate.

— 16 —

Prayer and Affirmation to
Neutralize, Heal, and Eliminate

HEARTACHE/HEARTBREAK

My Dearest, Most Holy Higher Self:
Today, I surrender all things to God.

I surrender the annoying little things, and the frightening big things, that cause me heartache.

I surrender every thought and belief; every bit of learning and programming; every mental and emotional construct; every ancestral, generational, and historical pattern of thinking; and every way of being that blocks, obstructs, hinders, delays, or denies my total reliance on and trust in the movement of God's Holy Spirit within me and on my behalf.

I surrender fear and anxiety, and all forms of worry, guilt, anger, frustration, impatience, stubbornness, arrogance, helplessness, and hopelessness that deny my total reliance on and trust in the movement of God's Holy Spirit.

I surrender attachments to all outcomes that I imagine, demand, fear, require, and attempt to control that have caused or could cause me heartache.

I surrender control, fear of control, lack of control, and all control issues that have caused or could cause me heartache.

I surrender my mind, my body, and my life into the heart of God.

I surrender my children and loved ones into the heart of God.

I surrender all forms of worry and regret about anything and everything I think, I need, I want, I require, I demand, and I expect into the heart of God.

I surrender by trusting You.

I surrender by praising You.

I surrender and affirm my knowing that the love of Your heart has set me free.

Today, my God, my Source, my Creator, I surrender my heart to You.

Fill my heart with love. Fill my heart with joy. Fill my heart to overflowing with the healing light of Your presence.

I ask! I allow! God becomes!

I let it be so, moment by moment!

And so it is!

Affirmation:

I surrender my heartache to God, and I am filled with the healing presence of God's love.

— 17 —

Prayer and Affirmation to Neutralize, Heal, and Eliminate

HELPLESSNESS/HOPELESSNESS

Precious Lord, My Father, My Mother, My Friend:

I come to You today seeking healing and the elimination of all thoughts, feelings, beliefs, behaviors, and generational and ancestral patterns that promote and support the spirit and experience of helplessness and hopelessness that has taken hold of me.

I come to You today to confess, heal, and eliminate all thoughts, feelings, beliefs, behaviors, and generational and ancestral patterns that have allowed me to believe that I am or have been stuck, trapped, defeated, overwhelmed, or incapacitated.

I come to You today to confess and acknowledge that You are the strength and power I need moment by moment.

I come to You today knowing that Your love can and will lift me from the snare of all false images, limiting thoughts, distorted beliefs, and harsh judgments I have held about myself and against myself.

I come to You today with faith, knowing and believing what You can do and will do in me, for me, and as me, when I ask and believe.

I come to You today asking to be healed, to be restored, to be renewed, to be refreshed, to be reminded, and to remember the total and complete truth of who I am.

I am the love of God, breathing, living, and moving by divine right.

I am the purposeful power of God, breathing, living, and moving by God's grace.

I am the wisdom of God, breathing, living, and moving as I open my mind and heart to greater, grander, and new possibilities.

I am the vision of God, breathing, living, and moving through life to uncover and discover the outcome I desire.

I feel a new way of being growing in me and as me.

Thank You, God, for lifting me above all thoughts, beliefs, behaviors, and generational and ancestral patterns of helplessness and hopelessness into the purposeful wisdom, love, and power that is now breathing, living, and moving in me and as me.

I let it be!

And so it is!

Affirmation:
God is my help. God is my hope. I now move forward with grace and ease.

— 18 —

Prayer and Affirmation to Neutralize, Heal, and Eliminate

HOSTILITY

Precious Lord:

Today I am ready to learn to accept that I can and am willing to practice the art of friendliness.

I choose to surrender all hostile thoughts and feelings to the practice of amicability.

I choose to surrender any and all meanness, anger, resentment, bitterness, and hostility so that I can practice kindness.

I choose to be healed of, lifted above and freed from anything and everything that promotes, supports, or advances the presence of hostility in my mind, heart, way of being, and life so that I will experience and express the joy of agreeableness.

I forgive myself for any hurt or harm I created for others with hostile thoughts, feelings, or behaviors.

I forgive myself for any hurt or harm I have caused myself with hostile thoughts, feelings, or behaviors.

I forgive myself for allowing myself to believe that hostility was more powerful than enjoyment of myself, of life, of love, of God, and of others in my life.

I now choose to know that I can celebrate God.

I now choose to know that I can celebrate myself.

I now choose to know that I can celebrate life and all of the wonderful goodness it offers me.

I now choose to know that I can celebrate the love and the goodness that is present in others.

I know that as I celebrate God in all things and all people, my mind, my heart, and my life are filled with joy.

I celebrate joy! I celebrate life! I celebrate peace! I celebrate love!

I celebrate myself!

I celebrate You, God!

Thank You for opening my mind to all that is worthy of celebration.

And so it is!

Affirmation:

The more I celebrate God, the more I am filled with life, love, and joy to celebrate!

— 19 —

Prayer and Affirmation to
Neutralize, Heal, and Eliminate

HUMILIATION

Oh Lord, My Lord:

Humbly and reverently I turn to You, asking for the restoration of my dignity and self-respect.

I feel deflated, defeated, and humiliated.

I feel the sting of embarrassment in my soul.

There is a part of me that believes this is only a temporary state of being. And there is another part of me that feels disgraced, disrespected, and wounded.

In this moment, I stretch my hands to You, asking for Your help.

In this moment, I stretch my hands to You, asking to be restored.

I lift my mind to You, asking to be strengthened.

I lift my heart to You, asking to be healed.

Humbly and reverently, I ask to be delivered from my ego self, which believes I have been denounced and destroyed.

I step into Your presence now, knowing my healing is assured.

I fall into Your love now, knowing that I am being renewed and refreshed.

I now sit in the light of Your presence, knowing that no hurt, harm, or darkness can enter where You and I are joined together.

Thank You, God, for the total and complete restoration I feel growing within me.

Thank You, God, for the peace I feel anchoring within me.

Thank You, God, for the joy I feel moving in me and through me, as it heals every fiber of my being.

I rest in Thee, God, claiming this restoration.

I rest in Thee, God, claiming all-abiding peace.

I rest in Thee, God, knowing that what may have been meant for my harm has brought me to this moment of love.

With a grateful and joy-filled heart, I rest in Thee.

Thank You, God!

Amen.

Affirmation:

God's plan is unfolding. God's power is working. I am secure in the presence of God.

— 20 —

Prayer and Affirmation to Neutralize, Heal, and Eliminate

HURT/WOUNDEDNESS

Dear God:

Today, I am taking a step to You, God.

Thank You for ordering my steps.

I acknowledge You as the source of my healing and wholeness.

I acknowledge You as the eternal presence of love and life within my being.

I acknowledge You as the comfort I seek, the support I desire, and the strength I need.

I acknowledge that as I step into Your presence, all things within me, about me, and for me are made right again.

Today, I am stepping away from the thoughts, beliefs, behaviors, people, situations, and circumstances that I believe have caused me hurt and left me wounded.

Thank You for ordering my steps.

Today, I step away from sorrow, suffering, humiliation, and all the false images that have blocked the truth of who I am with You and who You are within me.

Thank You for ordering my steps.

Today, I step away from all beliefs and judgments that have allowed me to believe that You are not guiding and protecting me from situations, circumstances, and people who could or have caused me hurt and left me wounded.

Thank You for ordering my steps.

Today, I step away from any desire, attempt, or attachment to control what others think, do, or say.

Thank You for ordering my steps toward healing.

Thank You for ordering my steps toward wholeness.

Thank You for ordering my steps toward You, God, and for reminding me that the protection of Your guiding light is always within me.

I am so grateful to have You by my side.

In joy, I now step forward with You.

And so it is!

Affirmation:

All wounds are now healed! I step away from hurt, knowing God is ordering my steps.

— 21 —

Prayer and Affirmation to Neutralize, Heal, and Eliminate

INADEQUACY/INCOMPLETENESS

Beloved Creator, My Precious Source of Life and Being:

In Your loving presence, I am aware of Your life within me.

In Your loving presence, I acknowledge the holiness of You within me.

In Your loving presence, I declare and decree I am enough, just as I am.

In Your loving presence, I affirm that I am whole and complete, just as I am.

There is nothing missing in me.

There is nothing wrong with me.

There is nothing that I cannot be, do, or have, as long as I remember who I am.

I am a divine demonstration of all that You are within me.

I am a unique representation of all that You are within me.

In Your loving presence, I reclaim and reaffirm the truth of who I am.

In the wisdom of Your presence, I declare and decree that I am enough, just as I am.

In the light of Your all-knowing presence, I declare and decree that I am enough, just as I am.

Every thought that I am anything other than enough is now banished and disintegrated.

Every belief that I can be less than I am is now eliminated at the deepest root and cause.

Every judgment, every learning, every projection I have made about myself, or against myself, now disappears into the sea of forgetfulness, never to rise again.

I declare and decree I am enough, just as I am.

I declare and decree I am enough, because You are in me and with me.

I declare and decree I am enough, just because I am.

I declare and decree that these words now take shape and form as the truth of my being, and I cannot be otherwise.

I am enough!

And so I am!

Amen and Amen.

Affirmation:

Who I am, just as I am, is enough for God and enough for me.

— 22 —

Prayer and Affirmation to Neutralize, Heal, and Eliminate

INDECISIVENESS

To You, dear God, I offer my mind and heart:

I acknowledge You as the ever-present, all-knowing presence of Infinite Intelligence.

I ask to be filled with the light of Your presence.

I acknowledge You as the eternal light of wisdom and peace.

I ask to be filled with the wisdom and peace of Your presence.

I acknowledge You as the stabilizing strength and purposeful power present in its fullness, at all times, in all places.

I ask to be filled with the strength and power of Your presence.

I declare that Your presence now fills me.

Knowing this, I surrender and ask to be healed of all thoughts and feelings that hinder my ability and right to choose.

As Your wisdom anchors within me, I know exactly what to do at all times.

I trust the all-knowing fullness of Your presence within me.

I surrender the fear of making a mistake.

I trust the presence of Your strength and power within me.

I make choices and decisions with grace and ease.

I think calmly and speak clearly in the sacred presence of my God.

Every thought I have is filled with and guided by the presence of God.

I remember and affirm the powerful presence of God within me.

I surrender all fear, knowing that God hears all, knows all, and gives all.

Now, I let it be.

For this awareness and understanding, I am so very grateful.

I let it be!

And so it is!

Affirmation:

I am in God's presence now. In God's presence, I know all that I need to know and all that I need to do.

— 23 —

Prayer and Affirmation to Neutralize, Heal, and Eliminate

INSECURITY/ SELF-CONSCIOUSNESS

My Precious Creator and Source of My Life:

I love You today.

I love You for all You are within me.

I love You for all You are through me and all You do as me.

I love and accept the realization that Your grace is my strength.

I love and acknowledge the understanding that Your love is my power.

I am aware and I affirm that Your wisdom is my guidance.

Acknowledging You and affirming this truth, I ask to be healed from all vestiges of insecurity and inferiority.

Acknowledging You as the essence of my being, I ask that all thoughts, beliefs, feelings, learnings, and attachments to the belief that I am, have been, and could be inferior now be dissolved and released from every fiber of my being.

I know the truth.

I am as You created me to be—precious and powerful, noble and divine.

Help me, precious Creator, to stand in the truth: that I am wonderfully made by You.

I acknowledge that You are my Source and the supplier of all my needs.

I acknowledge the mercy of Your forgiveness when I hold judgments about myself.

I acknowledge the peace Your presence brings when I feel insecure or unsafe.

I welcome the answers Your truth brings when I put my trust in You.

I love the joy Your love brings moment by moment.

I now ask that my entire being be filled with the presence of Your truth and love.

I give thanks and praise to You with the fullness of my being.

I let it be!

And so it is!

Affirmation:

I am secure in God's presence. I am secured by God's love.

— 24 —

Prayer and Affirmation to Neutralize, Heal, and Eliminate

JEALOUSY

Precious Lord, My Blessed Source:

I acknowledge Your presence and power at the core of my being.

I acknowledge You as the truth of my being and the strength of my life.

I acknowledge that the love You have for me can never be destroyed, diminished, or taken away.

Today, I press into Your presence and confess that I have been holding jealousy in my mind and heart.

I confess I have been unable to wish the best for others.

I confess I find myself in anger, sadness, and fear when I see the good that others have or the good that they do.

I confess I find myself holding ill will toward others.

I am aware that these thoughts and feelings are the result of unhappiness and discontent within myself and with my current experience in life.

I confess, know, and accept that the thoughts and feelings of jealousy are merely a reflection of how I feel about myself and that they have nothing to do with anyone or anything outside of myself.

I confess that I feel ashamed and sad about holding jealous thoughts and experiencing feelings of jealousy.

Today, I turn to You, my Source, the Creator of my life, so I can be cleansed, healed, and brought into balance.

Today, I ask for and open myself to remember the truth of who I am.

I ask for and open myself to recognize the truth of who You are within me.

I acknowledge and accept that the good things I see in others and desire for myself reflect Your will.

I acknowledge and accept that Your will of good for me cannot be stopped, taken, or diminished by what others do or have.

Humbly, with great reverence and forgiveness, I ask to be cleansed and healed from the affliction of jealousy so that my eyes will be opened to the glorious possibilities that lay ahead of me.

Help me to forgive myself and remind me that what You have done for others, You will also do for me and within me.

Fill me with trust today. Fill me with confidence today. Fill me with gratitude today.

Remind me that Your goodness is not limited or restricted.

Fill my heart with joy, peace, and love today by reminding me that Your grace and love for me cannot be taken by anyone.

I am so grateful that all I ever need to do is ask for what I need and want, believing that You will always answer.

For the truth I am remembering, the healing I am receiving, and all the good that is yet to come, I am so grateful.

As I press into Your presence, I say thank You.

I let it be!

And so it is!

Affirmation:

I bless others for the good they are and the good they receive, knowing God's goodness cannot be limited. God's goodness for me is mine.

— 25 —

Prayer and Affirmation to Neutralize, Heal, and Eliminate

JOYLESSNESS/DEPRESSION

Blessed Holy Spirit:

With reverence and humility, I invite You into my heart.

It is my desire and intention to know the fullness of You today.

It is my desire and intention to rejoice and be glad for this day.

I ask You, Holy Spirit, to free me from the mental shackles and emotional chains that have sentenced me to despair and robbed me of the presence of joy in my life.

I ask You, Holy Spirit, to remove from my mind and heart anything that delays, blocks, hinders, or obstructs the experience of joy in my life.

I ask You, Holy Spirit, for an outpouring of pure joy into every fiber of my being.

I ask You, Holy Spirit, for an infilling of pure joy into every aspect of my life.

I ask You, Holy Spirit to fill me with Your presence so that I will know how to experience and express joy and so that I will experience and express joy.

I ask that You give me great joy and encouragement today.

I ask that the joy of the Lord be my strength today.

I ask You, Holy Spirit, to so fill me with the light of Your presence that unspeakable joy becomes the state of my being.

In the presence of joy, I know that all darkness will be lifted from my mind.

In the fullness of joy, I know that all heaviness will be lifted from my heart.

I lift my mind, my heart, and my hands to joy, Holy Spirit.

Fill me with joy! Fill me with overflowing joy that I can feel.

Fill me with joy! Fill me with undeniable joy that will renew me, refresh me, and restore me to my right relationship with You.

I know that I need only to call and You will answer.

Thank You, Holy Spirit, for answering this call.

Thank You for an infilling and outpouring of joy.

I can feel my joy coming!

And so it is!

Affirmation:

The Holy Spirit now fills me with joy. I am so grateful! I am so blessed!

— 26 —

Prayer and Affirmation to Neutralize, Heal, and Eliminate
LONELINESS/LONGING

Blessed and Divine Holy Spirit:
I ask that You heal and transform my mind.

Transform every thought of loneliness and longing.

Transform every belief that makes me isolate and turn people away.

Transform the energy of my heart that makes me afraid to connect with You and with others.

Fill me with a sense of acceptance and acceptability.

Bring my every thought into alignment with Your presence so that I will know and feel connected to You, to everyone, and to everything.

Holy Spirit, You are welcome in my heart.

Transform my heart, Holy Spirit.

Erase every feeling, memory, and experience that has anchored thoughts and beliefs of loneliness in my heart.

Transform every condition, situation, and circumstance that motivates me to remove myself from opportunities and possibilities to know and experience loving connection.

Holy Spirit, transform me, heal me, open my heart.

Transform every part of me that tries to withdraw from goodness, joy, laughter, and love.

It is my deepest and most heartfelt intention to live a life of peaceful and harmonious connection to people.

Fill me with Your presence, which reminds me I am not alone.

Fill me with Your presence, which reminds me I never need to be alone.

Fill me with Your presence, which reminds me it is safe to be loved and connected.

Holy Spirit, You are welcome in my mind, my heart, and my life.

I accept and allow Your presence to be the courage I need to let others in.

For Your presence, Holy Spirit, I am so grateful.

Now, I let it be!

And so it is!

Affirmation:

I am infilled and fulfilled with the presence and safety of the Holy Spirit. I am safely connected to others.

— 27 —

Prayer and Affirmation to Neutralize, Heal, and Eliminate

LOST

Beloved Father God, Blessed Mother God:
I call forth the presence of Your Holy Spirit.

I call forth the presence of Your grace and mercy.

I ask for and open myself to receive the deepest level of healing available in every aspect of my being.

Give me clarity. Give me strength.

Give me a sense of direction and purpose.

I now surrender all limiting thoughts and beliefs.

I now surrender all doubt, self-judgment, fear, and confusion.

I now surrender any anger directed toward myself or another.

I now surrender thoughts and beliefs grounded in helplessness and hopelessness.

I now surrender any sense of feeling or being lost.

In the place of all that I surrender, I ask to be filled with the essence of confidence, self-assurance, divine guidance, and clarity.

*In the place of all that I release, I open myself to be
filled with love and compassion.*

*I allow myself to experience and express a strong and
unwavering sense of purpose, value, and belonging.*

*I claim my divinity and my inheritance as the beloved of
God.*

I claim my oneness with God and with all of God's power.

*I give thanks, dear God, for my divine connection with
You.*

I thank You for being a God of second chances.

*I affirm that I will now move forward easily, effortlessly,
under grace.*

*I am so grateful this prayer has been heard and is
answered.*

*I am so grateful for my renewed sense of direction and
meaning.*

*I look forward to finding new and exciting possibilities
and opportunities.*

I know my best is yet to come.

And so it is!

Amen.

Affirmation:

*Today, in the perfect healing presence of God, I move
forward with clarity, purpose, determination, and peace.*

— 28 —

Prayer and Affirmation to Neutralize, Heal, and Eliminate
LOW SELF-ESTEEM/ INFERIORITY

Dear God:

Today, I ask that the presence of Your love and power fill the words of this prayer so that I will be healed.

I have lost all sense of who I am and why I matter in life.

I have lost my sense of value, worth, and meaning.

I have lost the understanding of my authentic self, who I am in You, and I struggle with feeling less than You created me to be.

Today, it is my intention to seek, find, experience, and express my true self.

Today, it is my desire to live with a renewed sense of who I am.

I acknowledge my potential and inherent right to be uniquely me.

I consciously release all false versions of who I thought I was, and I consciously replace them with a deep and lasting connection to my authentic identity.

I no longer choose to compare myself to others.

I choose to see myself as You created me.

I choose to accept myself as a divine demonstration of all that is goodness and greatness.

I choose to focus my attention on using my time and talents to create a life that supports a greater unfolding of the best of me.

I acknowledge and choose to stand fully grounded in the power of who I am.

I see myself as whole, complete, competent, and divine.

I decree and declare that I matter to You, I matter to myself, and I matter to life.

Knowing that these words have been heard and received in the presence of God, I offer joyful praise and gratitude.

I let it be!

And so it is!

Affirmation:

Firmly, I stand in the truth of my being, knowing that I am filled and fulfilled by the power of my authentic identity. I matter!

— 29 —

Prayer and Affirmation to Neutralize, Heal, and Eliminate

NUMBNESS/ DISCONNECTEDNESS

Precious and Divine Holy Spirit:

I call for Your presence today, knowing that You are the movement and the activity of God, my Source, my Creator.

I call out to You today with an open heart.

I call out to You, asking with the willingness to receive an outpouring of Your essence so that I will feel the energy of love.

Holy Spirit, I have been numb, shut down, cut off, and disconnected from my Source.

I know that the spirit of God and the energy of love abides in my heart.

Holy Spirit, I confess that my heart has been closed. It has been cold. It has been hardened by situations and experiences I could not understand or accept.

I confess that I long to feel the joys of life, to enjoy a connection to people, and to share the essence and energy of my heart.

Holy Spirit, I confess I have been afraid, until today.

Today, I am willing to feel and to share my feelings and to connect with others from the depth of my being.

Today, I am willing to have my heart brought back into alignment with Your presence, knowing You are the essence of God's love.

Heal my heart today, Holy Spirit. Open my heart so that I will once again be connected to and experience the ebb and flow of life in the core of my being.

Open my eyes so that I will see and know the beauty of life beyond what is difficult, hard, and painful.

Wake me up. Shake me up. Reconnect me to the truth of what I feel and desire.

I call upon You, Holy Spirit, knowing in Your presence I am safe and protected.

I am ready to feel again. I am ready to love again. I am ready to live fully and experience life on all levels, with all people, at all times.

Holy Spirit, heal my heart at the deepest level available to me at this time.

Keep me safe in Your care.

I let it be!

And so it is!

Affirmation:

I am reconnected to life. I feel the presence, light, and love of the Holy Spirit moving in my heart.

— 30 —

Prayer and Affirmation to Neutralize, Heal, and Eliminate

OVERWHELM

Divine Spirit of Life, God, by All the Names You Are Known and Called:

I have taken on too much. I am doing too much.

Much is being asked and required of me.

In this moment, my mind and heart are overwhelmed, and I am leaning into You for support and relief.

You are the light in my soul.

You are the hope in my heart.

You are the creative essence of my mind.

You are the purpose of my life.

I will take a deep breath, slow down, and surrender all thoughts to You.

I surrender all thoughts of the past and future to You.

I surrender all of my cares and concerns to You.

I surrender all of my responsibilities and assignments to You.

I ask that You heal, transform, or eliminate into Your light all thoughts of "I can't" in my mind.

I ask that You transform into Your love any fear, restlessness, and obligation in my heart.

I ask that You transform into courage any hesitation in my thinking or my way of being.

Keep me on the path today.

Keep me in Your light today.

Carry the load for me today.

Be my strength now and forevermore.

I ask! I allow! God becomes!

Thank You!

And so it is!

Affirmation:
I rest in the presence of the Holy Spirit. I am completely revitalized as I rely on the perfecting presence of God.

— 31 —

Prayer and Affirmation to Neutralize, Heal, and Eliminate POWERLESSNESS

Blessed Father:

I give You my mind today, asking that You quiet all false ideas that have led me to believe I am powerless.

Grant me freedom from the mistaken ideas about who I am that motivate me to act as if I am powerless.

I declare today as the Holy Instant during which my mind was healed and brought into perfect alignment with the power of God. I know that God's power is my power.

I give You my heart today, asking that You eliminate, eradicate, and disintegrate any energy within me that has been created by toxic, unloving, unproductive emotions, memories, beliefs, and traumas that may in any way block, hinder, deny, or obstruct my ability to stand powerfully in my life and in the world.

I declare today as the Holy Instant during which my heart was healed and brought into perfect alignment with the will of God.

I give You my life today, asking that You guide me, lead me, instruct me, correct me, and remind me of Your presence within me, Your plan for me, and Your love of me.

I declare today as the Holy Instant during which all aspects of my mind, my heart, and my life were healed and brought into perfect alignment with the power and presence of God within me.

I am available to receive the fullness of Your presence.

I accept the gifts that Your power brings forward in me and as me.

I declare today as the time I will know, accept, allow, and believe that Your Holy Presence and all of its power is unfolding within me, through me, and all around me, moment by moment.

Today, I focus my complete attention and every intention on living as a loving and powerful demonstration of who You have created me to be.

I claim my power! I am grounded in my power! I am surrounded and supported by the presence of God's power.

As Your presence fills my mind, Blessed Father, I am so grateful.

Amen and Ache.

Affirmation:

God's power is my power. God's power is available and activated within me and as me.

— 32 —

Prayer and Affirmation to Neutralize, Heal, and Eliminate

PRIDE

Humble Me, Lord:

My mind, my heart, and my mouth have fallen prey to the pride-filled demands of my ego.

My thinking, my speaking, and my behavior have been inflated by my humanness to the point of overriding the call and needs of my spirit.

Forgive me for the aggressiveness of my thoughts, the harshness of my feelings, and the unkind and unloving ways in which I have behaved.

Forgive me for any hurt or harm I have caused to others.

Forgive me for the things I have said or done to promote, advance, and lift myself above and without consideration of You.

Humble me, Lord, so that I will live the true and loving fruits of my spirit.

Show me how to be. Correct me when I need it. Direct me according to Your plan and Your will for my life.

I now choose to be kind and loving. I now choose to be grace-filled and peaceful.

I now choose to be a representation, a demonstration, and an advocate for Your loving presence.

Help me, Lord, to see myself rightly and to behave in ways that are aligned with the truth of my soul.

Help me, Lord, to see others rightly and to treat them with the same loving compassion with which You have treated me.

Help me stand in and with the strength of my soul and not for the advancement of any selfish wants or desires.

Teach me when and where to stand up, when to sit down, how to speak up, and what to say for the highest good of everyone involved.

I just want to be better. I want to be a better person and a better demonstration of You.

Humble me, Lord, and heal my mind and heart of those things that move me away from Your presence and Your will.

I ask these things, knowing that every prayer is answered according to my trust, faith, and belief.

I trust You, Lord. I put my faith in You, God. I believe that You know my heart and my needs.

I give thanks right now for Your loving presence, which fulfills my needs.

And so it is!

Affirmation:
The fruits of the spirit within me are stronger than the demands of pride.

— 33 —

Prayer and Affirmation to Neutralize, Heal, and Eliminate

REGRET

Beloved Father, Blessed and Divine Holy Spirit:

I acknowledge and accept that Your grace is always with me.

I surrender all regrets.

There are no mistakes You hold against me.

I surrender all regrets.

There are no mistakes in Your love for me.

I surrender all regrets.

Your grace is forgiving and allows me to forgive myself.

I surrender all regrets.

When I forget all the good things I am created to be, Your grace guides me back to my center.

When I get lost in the stories manufactured by my ego, Your grace saves me from myself.

When I go my own way without first seeking Your divine guidance, Your grace protects me.

All those times I have made mistakes that could have been my downfall, Your grace kept me safe.

Those times when I did not reap the full consequences
   of what I was thinking or speaking, it was because
   of Your grace.

I surrender all regrets.

I have done nothing for which You would punish me.

Your grace is the unwavering and unconditional love
   You have for me.

It is Your grace for which I am so grateful.

It is the power of Your mercy for which I give You
   praise.

Thank You, God, for Your love.

Thank You, God, for Your grace.

Your grace has been and shall be my all sufficiency.

I now rest in Your grace.

I surrender all regrets.

I let all things be!

And so it is!

Amen.

Affirmation:
I surrender all regrets. Through thick and thin, no
matter what, God's grace will guide and keep me.

— 34 —

Prayer and Affirmation to Neutralize, Heal, and Eliminate

REJECTION

Father, Mother God, Blessed and Divine Holy Spirit:

I am offering You this prayer as my weapon to fight off thoughts and feelings of rejection.

You have promised me that no weapon formed against me shall prosper.

I have been in battle with feeling denied, pushed away, forsaken, and rejected.

I have been in battle—within my own mind—about why I have been discarded as unimportant.

Today, I am choosing my victory over these thoughts and feelings.

Today, I am choosing to remember that You accept me, You have a purpose for me, and You love me deeply.

Today, I am choosing to combat the thoughts and feelings of rejection with acknowledgment and acceptance of Your loving presence within me.

In my most difficult and dark times, You, God, have been there.

*When others have turned their backs and walked away,
You have been with me.*

*When I have felt lonely, when I have been exhausted,
when I was chasing human connection and affection,
You have whispered, "Come unto me."*

Your loving presence has never failed me. Your acceptance of me has never disappointed me.

*In this moment, I ask for a deeper and conscious
connection to You that will eliminate and heal what I
have called rejection.*

*Today, it is my intention to be fully aware, to accept and
acknowledge the presence of Your love.*

*Your love lifts me. Your love heals me. Your love
comforts me. Your love corrects all errors in my mind
and wounds in my heart.*

*Thank You for healing me of all thoughts, feelings, and
experiences of rejection.*

*Thank You for reminding me that with You and in You, I
can be loved beyond measure.*

*Thank You, God, for the presence of Your Holy Spirit that
has already answered this prayer.*

I feel Your presence now.

I rest in Thee.

And so it is!

Affirmation:

*God has never, can never, will never rejected me. I feel
the presence of God's love.*

— 35 —

Prayer and Affirmation to Neutralize, Heal, and Eliminate

RESENTMENT

Dear God, My God:

I invite You into every aspect of my mind today to heal me of resentment.

I invite You into every aspect of my heart today to heal me of resentment.

I invite You into every aspect of my life today to heal me of resentment.

Give me wisdom, dear God. Give me patience. Give me a new way of being so that resentment shall never again find a home within me.

I ask that the healing power of Your love and truth flow through me so that I will come into a divine understanding of every experience that has caused me to feel resentment.

I open myself fully to receive Your presence.

I open myself to be healed.

In Your presence, I surrender all thoughts of resentment.

I open myself to feel and express kindness and gentleness.

In Your presence, I let go of all resentments.

I open myself to feel and express acceptance and compassion.

In Your presence, I let go of my old ways of thinking and being that have allowed resentments to fester in my mind and heart.

I open myself to create new experiences for myself in every aspect of life.

In Your presence, I embrace and affirm love, acceptance, and peace.

Thank You, God, for surrounding me with Your light.

Thank You for filling me with Your love.

Thank You for reminding me of the truth.

There are no mistakes. I surrender all regrets.

I claim my freedom from resentment.

I am so grateful!

Thank You!

And so it is!

Affirmation:

The presence of God's wisdom and love in my soul now sets me free from all resentments.

— 36 —

Prayer and Affirmation to Neutralize, Heal, and Eliminate

SADNESS/SORROW

Blessed Divine Holy Spirit:

I acknowledge You as my Source and my strength, knowing that only Your presence can erase the sadness in my heart.

I accept You as my joy and my peace, knowing that with Your compassion the sorrow I feel will be lifted.

I am aware that You, the Source of my healing, will lead me back to wholeness.

Faithfully trusting the power of Your loving presence, I ask to be healed and lifted out of the sadness that has overtaken me.

I place the concerns of my heart in Your care today.

I place the heaviness of my heart in the care of Your love today.

I place all anxiety and worry about my life in Your light today.

I ask that You surround me with courage, infill me with comfort, and give me the peace of mind that will lift the burden of sadness from my heart.

I surrender my mind to You.

I surrender my heart to You.

I ask for the power of Your strength and wisdom to support me as I move through this temporary experience called sadness.

I am so grateful that I can lean on You to assist me.

I am so grateful that I can depend on You to do as I ask.

I am so grateful to know that You love me.

I am so grateful for Your presence, which will carry me to a new awareness and a new experience.

For You, Holy Spirit, I am eternally grateful!

I rest in Thee.

And so it is!

Affirmation:

I have found and reclaimed my joy in the presence of the Holy Spirit.

— 37 —

Prayer and Affirmation to Neutralize, Heal, and Eliminate

SELF-ABUSE

Precious Lord, Divine Father, Mother God:

I know that You created me with wisdom and love, and that all that You are, I am.

I know that You placed a calling in my soul and a purpose on my life, yet I feel I have missed the mark. There is a part of me that feels and believes I have disappointed You, and that part motivates me to engage in abusive behavior.

I confess, Precious Lord, that I have abused my mind and my body.

I confess that I have harbored abusive thoughts about myself, I have nourished abusive feelings toward myself, and I have engaged in abusive behaviors that threatened my well-being and my life.

I confess, Dear Lord, that I am powerless over these things, and I am turning to You for help and healing.

I am asking for the wisdom, strength, and courage to know myself, accept myself, love myself, and take care of myself.

I am asking for the presence of mind and peace of mind that I need to make better and healthy choices for myself.

I am asking for strength of will and discernment so that I'll know what is good, right, and best for me moment by moment, and how to choose rightly.

I am crying out to You as the Source of my life. I am reaching up to You as the foundation of my life. I am leaning into You as my help and my healing, moment by moment. I surrender my total being to You.

Protect me from the self-inflicted hurt, the mindless harm, and the dangers I face as a result of abusing myself. Wipe my slate clean so that I will be restored and renewed through the power and presence of Your loving-kindness.

Remove from me all thoughts and feelings that are not aligned with Your love of me and for me. Forgive me for everything I have thought, said, or done that stands in the way of my highest and greatest good unfolding.

I release the past easily and effortlessly into Your grace.

Thank You! Thank You! Thank You!

Let Thy will be done.

And so it is!

Affirmation:

I deny and denounce all self-abuse as I open myself to receive God's healing touch.

— 38 —

Prayer and Affirmation to Neutralize, Heal, and Eliminate

SHAME

I Praise You, God, as My Father, My Mother, My Friend:

I acknowledge that I am one with You.

I acknowledge that You are my wisdom and my peace.

I thank You for Your grace and mercy in every area of my life.

Breathe life into me, Father, so that the light of You will shine through me and eliminate all shame.

I now lift to You the broken places in my mind so that they might be healed of shame.

I now lift to You the broken places in my heart so that they might be healed of shame.

I now lift to You every mistaken thought—past and present—that has distorted how I see myself and filled me with shame.

I now lift to You every feeling I have held—past and present—that has polluted my heart with shame.

Light my heart with joy and fill my spirit with peace so that I will never again feel ashamed.

Give me total and complete acceptance of who I am on the inside, and let my acceptance of myself light up the world all around me.

I now reclaim the truth of my being in You. I now reestablish the power of my being in You.

I am so grateful that You know and accept me just as I am. I ask to be restored to the fullness of my identity in You. I now open myself for an outpouring of Your loving light and guidance.

Your spirit indwells me. Your truth infills me. Your love sustains me.

Your presence within me reminds me that I am totally and completely acceptable to You.

I declare there is nothing shameful about me.

Knowing that You are with me in all things and through all circumstances, I simply desire to demonstrate more of You as me.

Thank You, God, for reminding me who I am. Thank You, God, for teaching me to accept who I am. For this renewal and for the healing it brings, I am so grateful.

I let it be!

And so it is!

Affirmation:

I acknowledge and accept the presence of God in me as the truth of who I am that eliminates all shame.

— 39 —

Prayer and Affirmation to Neutralize, Heal, and Eliminate

STUBBORNNESS

Precious and Divine Holy Spirit:

I acknowledge that I am one with You.

I acknowledge that You are my wisdom and my peace.

I now lift to You the broken places in my mind so that they might be healed.

Create in me a gentle and cooperative spirit. I surrender all forms of stubbornness.

I now lift to You the broken places in my heart so that they might be healed.

Create in me a gentle and cooperative spirit. I surrender all forms of stubbornness.

I now lift to You every mistaken thought—past and present—that has distorted how I see myself.

Create in me a gentle and cooperative spirit. I surrender all forms of stubbornness.

I now lift to You every feeling I have held—past and present—that has polluted how I feel about myself.

Create in me a gentle and cooperative spirit. I surrender all forms of stubbornness.

*I now lift to You my behaviors—past and present—
through which I have labeled myself as wrong.*

*Create in me a gentle and cooperative spirit. I surrender
all forms of stubbornness.*

*I now lift to You all experiences—past and present—
that I have deemed as bad.*

*Create in me a gentle and cooperative spirit. I surrender
all forms of stubbornness.*

*I now lift to You every choice and every decision that
has taken my life away from the path of Your will.*

*Create in me a gentle and cooperative spirit. I surrender
all forms of stubbornness.*

I now reclaim the truth of my being in You.

I now reestablish the power of my being in You.

*I ask to be restored to the fullness of my identity in You,
with a calm, cooperative, and gentle spirit.*

I ask!

I allow!

*I accept as the Holy Spirit becomes this truth in every
fiber of my being!*

I let it be!

And so it is!

Affirmation:

*Who I am is anchored and secured in the flexible, coop-
erative, kindhearted, and receptive presence of the Holy
Spirit.*

— 40 —

Prayer and Affirmation to Neutralize, Heal, and Eliminate

UNAPPRECIATED/ UNIMPORTANT

Dear God:

My prayer today is simple: fill me with a spirit of gratitude.

I have given all I have to give and done more than expected of me, and my ego cries out to hear thank you.

Today, instead of wanting a thank-you from others, I am turning to You.

Fill me with a spirit of gratitude and thanksgiving.

Teach me how to be grateful for every blessing I have received.

Teach me how to celebrate every talent, gift, and ability I have used to support myself and others.

Remind me that every day I live to breathe again, to work, to laugh, to pray, to play, and to enjoy the gift of life as a blessing from You.

I confess there have been times when You have helped me, lifted me, saved me from my human condition, and I have forgotten to thank You.

*I surrender the need, the desire, the demand to be
recognized by others and ask for Your spirit of gratitude to fill and overtake me.*

*I am grateful, God. I am grateful to be alive. I am
grateful to be able to think and feel and make better
choices.*

*I am grateful for every lesson and every blessing I have
encountered and lived through.*

I am grateful for those who have been there for me.

*I am grateful to have been able to serve, support, and
assist others in their time of need.*

*I am grateful for my home, my health, and my ability to
do meaningful work.*

*I am grateful for every challenge and difficulty that has
helped me to become better, stronger, and wiser.*

So today, dear God, I ask that You hear my simple prayer.

*Fill me with a spirit of gratitude so that I will know and
remember that all I do, and all I give, is for You and
not for me.*

*Thank You, God, for hearing me. Thank You for loving
me. Thank You for working in me and as me.*

And so it is!

Amen.

Affirmation:
*I am filled with a spirit of gratitude for all that I am and
all that I have, and for all that I am able to do.*

— 41 —

Prayer and Affirmation to Neutralize, Heal, and Eliminate

UNSUPPORTED

Help Me, God!

I need to feel Your presence right now.

I am having a hard time.

I feel completely unsupported by those I expect to be there for me.

I have given to others, done for others, and been there for those who never seem to be there for me.

There is a part of my mind that knows You are holding me, lifting me, caring for me; there is another part of my mind that forgets.

So in this right-now moment, I am asking to feel Your presence so I will know I am being supported.

In this time of difficulty, let me know that You are with me.

Take the eyes of my mind off the need to have human support, and focus the energy of my soul on our divine support.

Help me to forgive those whom I believe have let me down.

Teach me to forgive myself for looking to others for the things I know I can get only from You.

Fill my mind with clear thoughts. Fill my heart with pure love.

Lift me from this pit of despair and let me feel Your presence in me and around me.

There is so much I desire to do. There is so much You have given me to do.

I am asking to know that I am supported, to feel supported, and to be supported so that I will complete every task and assignment with joy.

I thank You for the infilling of Your presence I feel right now.

I thank You for always, in all ways, being the support that I need.

I thank You for holding me by the hand, in the way only You can do, so that I will know and feel that I am always supported at all times, in all situations.

Thank You, God, for the privilege of this prayer.

Thank You, God, for the blessing of Your answer to this and every prayer.

I rest in Thee.

I let it be!

And so it is!

Affirmation:

I am so grateful that God is my ever-present and lasting support at all times, in all situations.

— 42 —

Prayer and Affirmation to Neutralize, Heal, and Eliminate

UNWORTHINESS/ WORTHLESSNESS

Beloved Holy Father:

Humbly I ask for, and gratefully I acknowledge, that Your loving presence is with me in this moment.

Teach me how to acknowledge my worth so that I will do so, as a divine expression of You.

Teach me how to accept my worth, so that I will do so, as a unique, creative expression of You.

Teach me how to appreciate my worth, so that I will do so, as a loving, purpose-filled expression of You.

Teach me how to live my worth, so that I will do so, as a creative expression of You.

Teach me how to demonstrate my worth, so that I will do so, as a courageous expression of You.

Teach me how to acknowledge, accept, recognize, embrace, appreciate, live, and demonstrate the awareness that I am worthy, so that I will do so, because of You.

Teach me how to acknowledge, accept, recognize, embrace, appreciate, live, and demonstrate the belief that I am worthy, so that I will do so, as a divine expression of You.

Today, it is my intention to embrace every opportunity to stand fully, powerfully, and boldly as a divine expression of the worth of God that I am.

God's life, as me, makes me worthy.

God's presence, as me, makes me worthy.

God's truth as me, makes me worthy.

God's love, as me, makes me worthy.

I surrender all limiting and self-denying thoughts, beliefs, and patterns of behavior.

I declare that I am worthy.

I surrender all thoughts, beliefs, feelings, and experiences that deny the truth of my being.

I declare that I am worthy.

I now ask the Precious Holy Spirit of life—the presence, movement, and activity of God—to give life energy to these words so that they will become the reality I live, moment by moment, for the rest of my life.

I thank You, Precious Spirit, for reminding me that this is so.

I let it be!

And so it is!

Affirmation:

I now acknowledge, accept, and appreciate how worthy I am as an individualized expression of God.

CHAPTER 8

THOUGHT THERAPY
IN REAL LIFE

*A thought is an idea, a premise, a conviction
that determines how you do, what you do,
when you do it, if you do it.*

—BISHOP T.D. JAKES

ne of the most difficult challenges for me as a minister, teacher, and spiritual life coach is to watch my clients and students suffer. Many folks have everything they need to create what they desire; they know what they need to do, and yet they don't do it. They suffer unnecessary stress because they won't meditate. They suffer from intolerable levels of worry and confusion because they won't pray. They suffer from issues of poor health and lack physical well-being because they refuse to eat mindfully or exercise minimally. The human brain's negativity bias, which wires us to give more attention to the negative than to the positive, means feeling bad can become so familiar that it almost feels good. Why people seem to be more content to complain and suffer than to consciously or consistently do what is required to improve themselves and their lives is a conundrum. Holding on to whatever or whoever is the source of our pain or distress is apparently much more comfortable than the effort required to get over it.

How do you travel the psychic distance from suffering (that is, living a life that stands in destructive opposition to your essence and your dreams) to liberation (in other words, living on purpose and making conscious choices every day of your life)? The shortest route from relentless suffering to triumphant liberation that I have ever witnessed has been through watching my students discover and deal with their dominant negative thought patterns.

Just as you eat and sleep every day to nourish your body and ensure its healthy existence, in order to maintain your psycho-spiritual well-being, you must build your GOI muscles.

WORTHLESSNESS

Climbing the Mountain

Mickie's journey from soul-deep suffering to freedom began when she attended a few of my classes with her girlfriend Shelia. Mickie had come of age in the dark shadows of her alcoholic father's verbal abuse and chronic unemployment and her mother's undiagnosed depression. Home was not a happy place. The women in Mickie's extended family, who always seemed to be lurching from one crisis to another, taught her not to expect much from life—in fact, she was programmed not to expect much *from* herself or *for* herself. When we met, Mickie had no vision for her life beyond making sure she got paid every two weeks by somebody, taking care of her two children, and praying that she would make it to the next paycheck or disaster—whichever struck first.

Mickie, who was always mistakenly considered to be "the quiet one," had hidden her core beliefs quite skillfully. Beneath her seeming compliance, she was a defiant ticking time bomb. Few people could have ever imagined the depth of Mickie's unexpressed rage. In most situations, Mickie was silent. She rarely stood out or stood up for herself. That was because Mickie had no voice. Her verbally abusive father had stripped it from her.

Mickie's hidden DNTPs were first outed by her friend. We were in class talking about what happens when we project our core beliefs onto people and things outside of ourselves. I had the group laughing about human beings' tendencies to act a lot like Dr. Jekyll and Mr. Hyde when they're unconscious. That's when Shelia recounted to the group the aftermath of one of Mickie's recent explosions.

Shelia said, "We were out shopping at a mall in a small clothing store for women. Mickie was quietly sorting through the sales rack and I was looking for a pair of earrings, when out of nowhere, I heard a loud voice reaming out the salesclerk who had been hassling a teenager about a jacket she was trying to return. I mean, it was *shocking*. Then I realized it was *Mickie* spewing the horrible insults and foul language. Mickie had gone straight 'Exorcist' on the clerk."

If you hurt someone whom Mickie cares about, or try to take advantage of someone who is weaker than you, quiet Mickie will go off. In these circumstances, Mickie's invisible fuse gets lit. Not only is she going to be seen, she is going to be heard! As I explained to the group, what concerned me most about Mickie's fireworks was this: suppressed core beliefs often contain multiple DNTPs that can lead to self-immolation *at a time when you can least afford to burn.*

After a year of getting to know Mickie through workshops and in a few one-on-one sessions, I discovered by accident that she was an amazing seamstress. She had made one of her classmates a wedding dress that included some of the most intricate hand sewing and beadwork I had ever seen. The gown was breathtaking—not only because it was form-fitted for a plus-sized woman, but because it was flawless. When the bride shared her wedding photos on her class-assigned vision board, she revealed that Mickie had made the dress for $150.

I was floored. The dress was clearly worth $2,500 or more, but that wasn't my real concern. I had been working with Mickie for months, supporting her in creating a vision for her life. With all the possibilities we had explored, all the ideas we tossed around, she never once mentioned that she could design and sew. When I pressed, Mickie explained that while growing up, she made all her own clothes because her family was so poor. She had learned how to reconstruct hand-me-downs so the other kids in school would stop making fun of her. She loved sewing but didn't consider it anything special because it was something that she had to do.

The 4A's to the rescue! The first step was to help Mickie become completely aware that what she was able to do with a piece of fabric was a special gift. She didn't recognize the fact that she could make more than "just a living" creating clothes for other people. I encouraged her to Google David Reisberg, the founder of David's Bridal, who began his empire making wedding gowns for family members and friends, just for the pleasure of it. He became a very wealthy man. After a few more coaching sessions and some homework assignments, Mickie discovered that her biggest challenge was charging people money. She didn't believe that she or her gift had any real value or that she had the right to charge people fair market prices for her creativity and labor. After I coaxed Mickie into watching an episode of *Project Runway* with me, I gave her an assignment: she was to watch an entire season of *Project Runway* and then give me a price for every garment created and presented on the show.

Mickie persevered and returned with a new awareness of the value of her skills and herself. Because she had never been formally trained, Mickie thought that she didn't have the right to charge people a lot of money for her clothing. During our conversation, Mickie remembered an unconscious DNTP that she had picked up from her mother. It was crude, irrational, and totally debilitating: "Who the f*** you think is gonna wear that sh** when they can get something better in a store." This is what Mickie's mother said to her when, at age nine, Mickie proudly displayed the first skirt she had made in school from an old dress her aunt had given her. She had used the old dress remnant because her mother refused to buy fabric for her school project. In her mind, Mickie had wired the value of her skills and work to her mother's rejection and her family's poverty. Although Mickie's teacher had told her that she was talented, Mickie was ashamed that her class assignments had to be sewn using surplus fabric the teacher gave her, and that those garments became her only school clothes. Unworthiness. Rejection. Shame. That was quite a collection of DNTPs for anyone to have to face.

Project Runway taught Mickie the value of her craft but did little to boost her self-worth. Although she had pulled herself up a few rungs by going to community college and becoming a medical coder and biller, she despised her life and herself. The generational DNTP she had picked up was this: life is hard, you're never going to have enough money to make it better, so you'd better hope you can find a decent man and keep him.

When Mickie reported for her coaching session and announced that she had broken up with the man she now referred to as her "lyin' and cheatin' live-in lover," she was hotter than an erupting volcano. That man was lucky to leave the relationship with his skin still attached to his body, and Mickie was finally so raw and so tired of suffering that she was willing to try anything. That's when we made a pact that Mickie would join one of my GOI focus groups.

In the GOI focus group, I explained to everyone that we all inherit "stuff" from our families of origin, ranging from the nuances of what we like to how we respond to certain people and experiences. Too often what we feel, hear, and see growing up becomes a subconscious 3-D game board of thoughts and feelings that too often create and direct our lives.

When the focus group participants had to identify their top four DNTPs, Mickie was still a little skeptical. But she remembered that using the 4A's as a new set of lenses for examining her past experiences had led her to a breakthrough and that the *Project Runway* assignment had given her a deeper awareness of her life's possibilities. She started to acknowledge how holding on to certain outdated core beliefs had led her to a dead end.

The beliefs that Mickie had made about her value and worth—the ones that led to decisions she was totally unaware of—were based on what she had seen, heard, felt, and experienced as a child. These were the bricks that created the foundation of her persistent and dominant negative thought patterns. Mickie was fighting against the DNTPs of unworthiness, rejection, shame, and rage, as well as the emotional scars caused by physical, psychological, and emotional abandonment.

Her awareness of herself as an individual, her needs, and her capacity to create a life in a meaningful, powerful, or productive way did not exist when she began her journey. At that point, Mickie was still a victim. She knew what had been done to her and not done for her, and she was angry about it. She didn't believe that she had a right to complain or speak out. So Mickie had commanded herself to be silent. She buried her real thoughts and feelings until—like a pressure cooker with too much heat—she finally blew up! When the invisible, silent Mickie morphed into "Exorcist" Mickie, everyone ran, which only reinforced her fear of abandonment. Slowly and with great care, I began to help her see how what she was thinking and feeling was showing up in her life.

In one class, I challenged Mickie to keep a negative thought journal for 90 days. Fewer than 30 days in, she got it. She became aware of how the thoughts she held about herself were showing up in her life. She finally began to see how her DNTP of worthlessness had landed her with a "sorry-ass, son-of-a-bitch, lyin' and cheatin' live-in lover." Initially, Mickie used that information to beat herself up, to make herself wrong.

"I can't believe what a fool I've been," she cried. "If fool me once is shame on you and fool me twice is shame on me, what happens when you fool yourself again and again and again? That must mean you're just a fool!" Self-recrimination is a common challenge when people bump into a new awareness about themselves. They judge themselves for what they did even when they were unaware that they were doing it. I tell them exactly what I told Mickie: it is unkind and unloving to expect yourself to know how to do something that you were *never taught* how to do.

Acknowledgment was a huge hurdle for Mickie. It took her quite a while to own her rage toward the long list of men who had lied to and betrayed her, starting with her father. The real difficulty came when she had to face the countless ways that she had abused herself for not being strong enough to fight back and defend herself as a child. Her core belief of worthlessness left her trying to prove her worth to herself by cycling in and out of relationships with men who violated, betrayed, and abused her. This resulted in her feeling even more unworthy, ashamed, and rejected. Every DNTP is the result of thoughts, feelings, and behaviors that dominate our consciousness due to constant repetition. Mickie had been reinforcing her negative beliefs about herself for a lifetime, and yet a healthy muscle hidden in her consciousness was beginning to reveal itself.

After the *Project Runway* assignment, Mickie started to want more for herself. She wanted her children to be better and accomplish more, too. She didn't want them ever to feel ashamed or abandoned. Initially, the thought of challenging her hidden DNTPs seemed overwhelming to her. She said she didn't know if she could survive the long, slow, painful process of healing. It took a lot of work, discipline, and even more self-compassion to help Mickie dig out of the pit of shame, blame, and betrayal.

Fortunately, Mickie's greatest asset was her willingness to change. However, when I introduced the concept of healing her DNTPs with the thought therapy tools of prayer and affirmation, she had an intense reaction. In her mind, the people who had treated her the worst of all when she was growing up were the people who, she said, "pretended to be Christians." That's when Mickie and I agreed that maybe a little more practice was in order. She needed to make the connection between intention and action in a very concrete way before we started her daily GOI work.

So, I gave Mickie a new assignment: a 45-day kindness project. Every day, for 45 days, she had to do three acts of kindness for someone she didn't know, then record what she had done in her journal. She could hold the door for someone, put money in an expired parking meter, give a stranger a compliment, help someone with her grocery bags, or anything else she could think of in the moment. The thing I loved about Mickie was that whenever I gave her an assignment, she would look at me, cock her head to one side, and say, "You know you are crazy as hell, right?" Then she would go off and do exactly what I had asked of her.

When Mickie returned with her journaling assignment, she had several remarkable stories of the wonderful things that had happened for her. She got a raise. She met a man, a really nice man. Someone—a stranger—had offered to sell her his house if she could move in within the month; he was being relocated by his job and had to leave in 10 days. She was amazed by the results of the project and was still fighting through disbelief.

I pointed out to Mickie that no one had refused her gift of kindness because she'd been verbally abused by her father or emotionally abandoned by her mother. Everyone who had been touched by her kindness had received it as a gift, a blessing, without even knowing about the mistakes she had made in choosing men or raising her children. Every act of kindness or giving comes from our God-ness, the goodness that exists within each one of us. That place cannot be touched by anything you do or don't do, nor is it affected by what happens to you on the level of physical experience. That sacred place within grows and expands alongside our consciousness. Mickie's acts of kindness started to reprogram her mind with positive dominant thoughts and prepared her to pry her mind loose from the generational DNTPs that had crippled her mind.

After her kindness assignment, healing her DNTPs with prayer and affirmations no longer seemed so weird. Mickie accepted this so-called thought therapy and started to use the GOI tools and process daily to create an amazing new life for herself. She realized that there was nothing that she could not be, have, or do once she got her mind right. Mickie was, in fact, truly joyous when we last hugged and kissed during a GOI class reunion.

She reported that she had quit her "good job" and was doing design work full-time and that she had two assistants. "Once I started working my GOI process, I felt like the spirit had blessed me with superpowers," Mickie said, laughing.

"Oh, so all of your problems and insecurities just disappeared?" one of Mickie's classmates questioned.

"Hardly," Mickie replied. "There is no magic fairy dust. The difference is that now I'm familiar with the DNTPs tools and process and I'm 'wide a-woke.' Now, whenever I start to feel stressed, or when I'm feeling upset over how situations are going or how people are treating me, I stop myself dead in my tracks and either do five minutes of conscious breath work or a few minutes of the thymus thump to calm myself down. Then I pull up the list of 42 DNTPs on my phone and speed-read it. If I can identify the DNTP because it's really obvious, I go to my daily practice outline and go through the steps. If I need more time to figure out my DNTP, my life preserver is the Universal Clearing Prayer."

Mickie was one of the first students to work through the entire GOI thought therapy process. Today, there are many, many more.

The following stories relate the GOI experiences of several individuals who have successfully engaged in thought therapy. I'm hoping after reading them you will be inspired to take a test drive. After all, what do you have to lose? The worst that could happen is that you try the process, it doesn't work, and you end up right where you currently are. If, on the other hand, you try the process and more light, more love, more peace, and a greater sense of well-being are facilitated in even one area of your life, then you will have no one to thank but yourself. That would make me happy and fill my heart with joy, and probably yours, too. So read these real-life stories and give thought therapy a try. Know that there are many others on the GOI path cheering you on.

ANXIETY / WORRY / FEAR

It Manifested as Procrastination

At the start of our GOI focus group, I said that if I could "get over" anything, I'd want to get over procrastination. What kind of procrastinator was I? I was the kind who started things and then didn't finish them or just took too long to finish them. I'd get excited about doing a project, and then somewhere along the way I'd drop it and make excuses as to why I didn't have time to complete it. I was inconsistent in multiple areas of my life, and that was very frustrating for me and for everyone around me.

I wanted to be able to follow through on things and be dependable. But for some reason, I'd wait until the last minute to tackle things that I knew about way ahead of time. It seemed like I wasn't fully involved until I was just about to miss the first deadline. Sometimes I got stalled due to a lack of clarity, and that kept me from moving forward; other times I got flooded with so many thoughts whirling around in my mind that I couldn't take action. And then sometimes I'd write out a list of notes for myself and I'd follow my list somewhat, but as I kept adding more and more items, I found myself stuck in a big ditch of overwhelm. Then I tended to (1) do nothing, (2) do only part of what was required, or (3) wait till the very last minute to get started and completely miss the deadline for what was supposed to be done.

What I really wanted to do was to get unstuck and move forward with the joy of completion and consistency. Then I could live my life on purpose instead of always having to make excuses that disappointed other people and myself.

So just what DNTP was in charge of my procrastination show? Some friends asked me whether I was afraid of success or afraid of failure. When I reviewed the DNTP symptoms for failure/frustration, they didn't ring true for me. However, when I read the explanations under anxiety/worry/fear, I could see myself very clearly.

Once I confirmed that my number one DNTP was anxiety/worry/fear, believe it or not, I started to feel better. There was a lot of relief in knowing that if I was a prisoner of procrastination, anxiety/worry/fear were my handcuffs. The GOI definition of anxiety/worry/fear felt very familiar to me: "Complete overwhelm; an inability to face or handle what may be required." The feelings presented in the "In Other Words" section sounded exactly like my real-life experiences: "You feel as if you're about to jump out of your skin, and you're not sure why. Your imagination is running wild about what happen or may not happen . . . This sense of being out of control and anticipating harm causes you to procrastinate or hesitate." And of course, I had my own "Internal Dialogue" lines that paralleled the ones in the DNTP list. "Did I turn off the stove?" "Does my boss hate me?" "Did I finish the report in enough time?" "Because I was late for the meeting, everybody thinks I'm incompetent."

On Day 1, my intensity level for anxiety was an 8. I thought it would be a 10 until I realized that I didn't have any pressing deadlines at work that day. I bookmarked my thought therapy prayer and affirmation, used the conscious breath work when

I did the silent prayer, and used the thymus thump when I spoke the prayer and affirmation aloud. Whenever I repeated the thought therapy affirmation throughout the day, I used the thymus thump. I was slightly nervous to measure my evening DNTP intensity level, but I was pleased to see that it had decreased to a 4.

On Day 2, my intensity rating started at 5. I repeated each of the steps in the GOI process and recorded my affirmation on my cell phone because a friend had mentioned that if you record an affirmation and play it back in your own voice, it's much more effective. There was something very empowering and healing about hearing my own voice speak the words of the antianxiety affirmation: "Boldly, I stand in the peaceful freedom that dissolves all anxiety, confusion, worry, and fear."

When an unexpected deadline was sprung on me, I used my affirmation and conscious breath work to shift my discomfort. Was it my imagination, or did I finish the assignment ahead of time?

My first venture into the GOI practice did require a few adjustments. I had to remember to do the sequences at the prescribed times. If I did the morning and forgot the afternoon, I'd continue the process for the rest of the day. However, when I followed the daily practice regimen each day at the prescribed times, I could feel a big difference in how my day played out.

When I woke up on Day 4, I felt like a huge boulder had been lifted from my shoulders because my DNTP intensity level had been reduced to a 2. It was the first time in a long time that I didn't feel like jumping out of my skin when I was faced with multiple deadlines. I decided to continue working with what I called my "anti-anxiety thought therapy process" for seven more days.

Over the next week, I found I had gained a lot more confidence in myself, and I didn't get as anxious or fearful when I had to make important decisions. My intensity levels fluctuated a lot over the week, but every evening the number steadily decreased. I also noticed that I no longer overreacted when other people around me started to get upset. No matter how my day went, I always made sure I used the thought therapy energy-clearing tools—conscious breath work, thymus thump, and thought therapy eye movements—in the evening or whenever I experienced an anxiety signal in my body. I can now recognize the early signs of anxiety, worry, or fear as distinct energies in my body. This is a new experience and a huge help because it allows me to identify the problem early on so it doesn't spiral out of control and leave me paralyzed or incapable of completing what I set out to do.

Since I started using thought therapy, no matter what was going on at work or what I need to accomplish, I have some tools that will help me clear any obstacles. I keep my daily affirmation posted on a sticky note at my desk so I can read it while talking on the phone or whenever I start to feel anxious. Now my coworkers want to know why I'm more productive these days!

The GOI thought therapy process has been a game changer in my life. Now that I'm aware of my procrastination triggers, I can immediately reel them in with my thought therapy tools. I've noticed that all of this has made me much more confident in my decision-making. I guess because my hidden DNTP is no longer running the show.

Doing thought therapy has been a very healing experience. I'm not the same person. I am, in fact, ready to take the steps required to move my life forward in a new direction. The GOI experience has opened up new spaces in my life, especially in my side hustle—the wellness business that I want to start. I'm getting more orders for my bath products every day, and I'm excited about that. I no longer count myself as a procrastinator because thought therapy has neutralized my number one DNTP. The result? This procrastinator has become an entrepreneur!

ANGER / RAGE

Anger Dishonors You

How do you "get over" loss? My sister, who was also my best friend, died unexpectedly on Mother's Day two years ago. I still haven't come to terms with that. I haven't spoken to my eldest son, a soldier deployed in Afghanistan, in more than a year. But my most devastating loss occurred recently when my husband of 15 years confessed that he's addicted to having sex with prostitutes. After we sought marriage counseling together, he announced in June that he's leaving me for another woman. This train wreck has been the most nightmarish experience of my entire life. On some days I thought the horrible pain and emptiness that was eating me alive would never go away. In fact, I felt paralyzed until I joined the GOI focus group.

Iyanla made the thought therapy process sound so simple. First, we would read through the master list of DNTPs and identify the descriptions that sounded most like us. Our feelings would be mirrored back to us in the "In Other Words" section, and the "Internal Dialogue" section would reflect the thoughts that race around in our heads all day long on repeat. Then we would identify the DNTP that we wanted to clear.

As I read through the list, I hovered over the DNTP for grief. I was, indeed, consumed with "intense emotional

318

suffering caused by loss, disaster, misfortune": the loss of my sister to cancer, the estrangement with my son, and the tragic end of my relationship with my husband—they all qualified as "intense emotional suffering." Was grief what I was experiencing? I identified with the descriptions—Do you feel "depleted" and "doomed?" Do you feel robbed of "your sense of meaning and purpose?" Do you believe that "nothing matters" anymore? Or say to yourself, "I just want to die!"?

Given the trickiness of our subconscious minds, what was the best way to identify our top DNTPs? Iyanla told us to ask ourselves, "What do you want?" That forced introspection unleashed a flood of uncensored thoughts, emotions, and journal work. What I wanted most in my life was to have a fresh new start. I wanted to take back control of my mind. I wanted to stop complaining about my problems. I wanted to stop letting my problems define me.

As I was about to settle on working with grief, another DNTP kept whispering to me: betrayal. The DNTP definition of betrayal fit perfectly. "Violation of integrity; broken trust . . ." "Deception . . ." "Disappointment of hopes or expectations." And the "In Other Words" section wouldn't stop ringing in my ears. "Someone you trusted and cared about threw you under the bus and then backed up over you." The "Internal Dialogue" words were also on point: "I trusted them, and they lied to me." "They exploited me." "They deceived me" in every way possible.

When I began to examine my "betrayal" intensity level, it was off the charts. It was a 10+, but Iyanla had reminded us that if a DNTP intensity level was higher than 10, it was still a 10. She also emphasized the importance of calming down your nervous system if your intensity level was above 10. I experimented with using conscious breath work while I asked myself, "What do you want?" Then on one long exhalation, the answer rushed out, "I don't want to be in a constant rage. I'm tired of being angry all the time."

Even as I acknowledged my husband's betrayal and my anger, the thought that kept popping back into my mind was that underneath all these thoughts and emotions was a well of unexpressed grief. I knew intuitively, though, that if I was ever to get over my grief, I first had to express my anger.

That reflection sealed the deal for me; anger/rage would be the first DNTP for me focus on. After all, it was a 10+. Iyanla acknowledged that even though my husband's betrayal was a radioactive issue for me, based on my original story, I may benefit most from working with my anger/rage—that it might be the master key that would unlock not just one door but many doors.

With my 10+ intensity level in hand, I started to antidote my anger/rage with the prescribed thought therapy prayer and affirmation. As I read the words of the prayer silently and out loud that first evening, I started to tremble:

> *I ask that You remove from me all vestiges of anger and rage, in all of their forms, at their deepest root and cause.*
>
> *You are the power in my life.*
>
> *Any power I have or express comes directly from You.*
>
> *Because You live within me, any experience or expression of anger dishonors You.*

Suddenly, my mind shifted. I was no longer my husband's or my son's victim; I was no longer God's victim. I was God's child. God was offering me a fresh start. If I could give up my anger with my sister for leaving me and my anger at my husband and son for not being who I wanted them to be, I could begin again.

The more I worked with the thought therapy energy-clearing tools—whether it was the conscious breath work, the thymus thump, or the thought therapy eye movements—I could feel my energy shift inside and outside. The heaviness that had plagued my spirit started to lift. I could breathe freely again. After that first deep breath, I swore to myself that I was going to stop living in the past; I was going to live in the present moment and claim every day as a fresh start.

My fresh start did not mean that all my dramas just disappeared. They did not. But every morning and evening when I completed the GOI thought therapy process, I had a renewed level of energy as well as the strength to endure whatever the day brought.

The thought therapy prayer and affirmation helped me deal with my life's tests in new ways. It was miraculous to make it through the day with some peace of mind. What I noticed most was that I no longer allowed myself to take everything so personally or to get upset so quickly. And the only things I had done differently were to say a little prayer and thump my thymus. I loved the thought therapy affirmation, too. *"Anger and rage are my enemies. I give myself permission to lovingly release all anger now."* Every time I repeated the words "anger and rage are my enemies" I realized that when I was unconscious, I had made anger and rage my best friends. My greatest new awareness is that life's inevitable troubles and difficult people do not have to control my life, my joy, or my happiness. I choose to depend on God every day. My strength and my peace are in Him.

On Day 4 of working with the anger/rage DNTP, the same day that I reached a morning intensity level of 0, I had to face a difficult situation with my soon-to-be ex-husband. He came to my house and tried to force me to have sexual relations. When I refused him, he took my car in retaliation, and I had to call the police.

Although the police couldn't resolve the situation because the car was in both of our names, the situation prompted me to get a restraining order. Even though I was afraid, drawing that firm boundary restored my inner peace. The thought therapy helped me manifest more courage than I ever thought I possessed.

The lines of the prayer allowed me to align with the divine:

Thank you, God, for the way You show up to clear, cleanse, and heal me.

I ask! I allow! God becomes the healing and the peace I desire.

My healing? On August 3, I stopped worrying about my husband—and my car. I purchased a new one. This was a deeply fulfilling moment for me because what the enemy had presented for my bad, God had turned around for my good. As long as I keep God first in my life and in my thoughts, and I surrender to the Holy Spirit, life's challenges will not get the best of me. I am blessed, and my life is a blessing. Nothing and no one can deter me.

As the prayer says: *Thank You, God, for being more powerful than any thoughts of or beliefs about my right to hold on to anger.*

INADEQUACY / INCOMPLETENESS

A $5 Net Worth

I have been working on financial freedom all my adult life, and while I have made "good money," I have never been financially literate. When Iyanla asked, "What do you want to 'get over'?" my answer was immediate: "Financial illiteracy!"

Due to my financial illiteracy, I was living in a situation that was increasingly unhealthy, and my relationship with a close family member was deteriorating. I could make money, and I could spend money, but in other respects my financial ignorance had become a tax that I could no longer afford to pay. Iyanla's second question was "What do you *really* want?" I understood that my money thoughts had a lot to do with what I knew and experienced around finance. Iyanla said that the thoughts that run our lives are mainly subconscious—that's why they never change. So even though I'd done lots of "work" around money, something was still terribly wrong with my money thoughts. I wasn't at all happy with my results. What did I want? I wanted to change my subconscious thoughts about money. I just had no map for getting to my subconscious thoughts about money. But I believed if I could learn how to reverse those thoughts, the result would be life changing.

After getting laid off from my job last spring, I decided that rather than go back to a nine-to-five job, I was going to use my skills to create something different for myself. After all, we were no longer in the old economy. I had skills and drive and financial necessity; I had to take care of my family—my young son, my mother, and myself.

Enter Iyanla's GOI focus group. When I was tapped to participate in the group for her latest "spiritual technology" called thought therapy, I was all in. Rather than just doing energy work or reciting prayers and affirmations, Iyanla had created a process for transmuting our hidden thought demons. First, she showed us how to identify our DNTPs; then, she introduced us to the five practical tools that we could use to neutralize them. If my subconscious thoughts were at the root of my financial suffering, and Iyanla was offering a new way to call them out of the darkness into the light, I was ready.

As a thought therapy focus group participant, I chose two DNTPs, as requested: inadequacy/incompleteness and anger/rage. My showdown with inadequacy/incompleteness revealed my own personal sinkhole. I followed the daily thought therapy process Iyanla had outlined, which meant that I used the energy transmutation tools of conscious breath work and thymus thump and then recited the prayer and affirmations each morning and evening. Iyanla said that most patterns could be cleared by committing to a total of 30 to 60 minutes a day (depending on whether you did the journaling work or not) in two to five daily sessions.

My intuition told me that I needed to do the work for three weeks, even though we had to commit to only two weeks. Following my intuition produced the desired results because by working with this process, I was able, subtly and over time, to identify my subconscious thoughts of inadequacy around wealth and abundance. I began to recognize that, when it comes to the energy of money, I had been afraid to stick even my big toe into the unlimited stream of wealth and abundance. Rather than fully partaking, I had been holding myself back because of a hidden core belief that I was undeserving of anything more than just what I "needed." How can you claim abundance if you can commit to receiving only "just enough" and not one dollar more?

As I engaged the thought therapy process, I realized that even with all the money work I had done over the years on abundance/lack, I still felt out of my league when it came to wealth. I discovered I still didn't have a wealth consciousness; I was wallowing in a subconscious poverty consciousness. I was reminded that when poor people come into unexpected money, they can never sustain it.

As I worked with the thought therapy prayer and the affirmation for inadequacy, I began to see that my thoughts and subsequent feelings were related to my sense of what value I saw attached to myself. The DNTP definition and the "In Other Words" section reflected my experience: "You just don't measure up. Comparing yourself to others, you can see what they have or are capable of and what you don't have or aren't capable of. You feel less than others, and you either highlight your shortcomings or shrink back to hide them. In the worst-case scenario, you keep trying to prove to others— and to yourself—how great you are, even when you don't really believe it."

Sometimes my hidden DNTP's "Internal Dialogue" felt like an MP3 player stuck on permanent repeat. "I never measure up." "Something is wrong with me." "I better not say . . ." "I just don't have what it takes." "There's something missing in me." "Why do I feel so incomplete?"

I did not feel worthless; but I just knew that something had been subtracted from my total value long before I was born. Using the thought therapy journal prompts, I reflected on my literal and psycho-spiritual experiences. And because I have been an avid journaler, I used the original questions as a springboard to dive deeper into my thoughts and feelings. I wanted to see how deeply these hidden thoughts had impacted and shaped my financial reality.

Even though we were asked to test Iyanla's spiritual technology for two weeks, I was committed to manifesting a breakthrough. I kept pressing on with the prayer and affirmation and the conscious breath work and the thymus thump and thought therapy eye movements for an additional week because I knew my money story went way, way, way back.

The more I journaled, the more I discovered how my thoughts around my family and the family's generational history affected how I saw myself. My thoughts and feelings about my so-called market value had been coded into my DNA through the stories of my mother, my mother's mother, my mother's mother's mother far beyond America and all the way back to Africa, when my ancestors' mothers had been reduced to commodities to be bought and sold.

Previously, had you ever told me that it was this ancient history and not everyday 21st-century inequality that determined my relationship with wealth consciousness, I would have certainly argued with you. Having our value determined by an outsider, having no say about who we were and what our value was, had impacted me just as much as it had impacted my forebears. This subconscious inheritance had affected my financial literacy, just as it would impact my son's if I did not heal it right here and right now. My forebears had guaranteed that future generations of our family would exist; now I had to ensure that my "future generation"—my child—had the ability to thrive. That could happen only if I was able to instill in my mind a new money consciousness, one that I could plant and nurture in his mind, too.

Even today, others are still determining my value. When I did a Google search for "worth and black women," article after article confirmed that the average single black woman's median net worth in America was $5! Talk about dominant negative thought patterns!

Identifying the specific DNTPs and using the thought therapy tools to transmute them broke through the glass ceiling that had imprisoned my mind. Today, my awareness of these programmed thoughts is easier to see, and I can recognize the results. I'm aware that I have approached the flow of money in my life with a thimble. Thus, I was getting only a thimbleful of God's limitless resources in return and trying to make myself believe that was all I deserved.

After the thought therapy work, I can confront hidden fears and anything that triggers my DNTP of inadequacy that has been holding me back from manifesting what I deserve. I no longer subconsciously have to buy the collective money DNTPs that surround black women and women of color. I can define myself in a new way and create a new reality for myself. I'm aware of the lesson that identifying my DNTP has shown me regarding the energy of money and how it relates to me.

I found these lines from the prayer to be very empowering:

> *In Your loving presence, I declare and decree I am enough, just as I am.*
>
> *. . . Every thought that I am anything other than enough is now banished and disintegrated.*
>
> *Every belief that I can be less than I am is now eliminated at the deepest root and cause.*
>
> *Every judgment, every learning, every projection I have made about myself, or against myself, now disappears into the sea of forgetfulness, never to rise again.*
>
> *I declare and decree I am enough, just as I am.*
>
> *I declare and decree I am enough, because You are in me and with me.*
>
> *I declare and decree I am enough, just because I am.*
>
> *I declare and decree that these words now take shape and form as the truth of my being, and I cannot be otherwise.*
>
> *I am enough!*
>
> *And so I am!*
>
> *Amen and Amen.*

I knew that inadequacy was the right DNTP for me to focus on, as opposed to working on my sense of worth, because the voice in my head was practically quoting from the "Internal Dialogue" script. I could make money, and I could work with money. But I could not make money work for me. I just couldn't measure up in terms of my financial literacy. I had never been able to see the results of money earned or spent unless it was to take care of my family's most basic needs—even though I desired more . . . much, much more. Iyanla told us we could read how successfully we had deprogrammed our DNTP by looking at what was showing up in our lives.

I began to experience the following life reflections: money that I could have sworn I spent was still in my bank account. Then, the registration for an online course that I wanted to take was about to close, and I was short the class fee. In my new commitment to financial literacy, I refused to resort to my emergency charge card. I was disappointed but content. Then, out of the blue, a good friend called hours before the course closed to tell me that she would gift me two months tuition because she was certain that with my new mind-set I would be able to create the outstanding balance due. And at the time of this writing, my mother alerted me she had a lead on a new-used car for the price of four new tires and a water pump!

But the biggest confirmation of the energetic shift that I experienced came when I took my darling science-geek tweenager to see the movie *Hidden Figures*. The DVD liner notes describe the film as the "untold true story of the brilliant African American women at NASA who served as the brains" that turned the tide in America's space race. It expressed to me in no uncertain terms that even when you know that you have worth, you can still get tripped up if you have one or more invisible DNTPs running in the background. Fortunately, these heroic women refused to accept the inadequacy DNTP of their day, and the rest is American history. As I could now explain to my son, the outer always reflects the inner, and once you deprogram your mind, there are no limits.

CHAPTER 9

AT THE END OF THE DAY

*It is impossible that anything should come to me
unbidden by myself. Even in this world, it is I
who rule my destiny. What happens is what I desire.
What does not occur is what I do not want to happen.
This must I accept.*

—LESSON 253, *A COURSE IN MIRACLES*

esson 253 from *A Course in Miracles* may seem like a bitter pill to swallow; however, until and unless we accept and acknowledge the divine and creative power of the mind, we will remain victims of our history, experiences, judgments, false perceptions, and the DNTPs that grow from the same.

You are the only one who gets to say what goes on in your life. It begins with the thoughts you entertain and engage in on a moment-by-moment basis. I learned this the hard way, through great physical suffering and emotional turmoil. I learned this by accepting and acknowledging my personal power after I became aware of the creative energy of my mind. If a thought could create a car, an airplane, a multimillion-dollar corporation, or a computer, why couldn't I use my mind to create peace in my day and prosperity in my purse? There was absolutely no reason, other than the way I thought about what I thought about.

"People don't do anything unless there is a reward or a benefit attached to it. No matter how good your offer may be, it's got to be a better deal than the one they already have on the table," advised one of my favorite teachers. I hope I can persuade you to take me up on my offer of thought therapy. It's a much better deal than suffering.

Many of the people who come to my classes and workshops believe that they are ready to begin the process of getting over what they have experienced. Yet they are totally unaware of and resistant to accepting any responsibility for their lives. They remain hell-bent on blaming others and projecting their emotions outward rather than acknowledging that their ongoing unconscious behavior has set them up for either a monumental breakdown or a major breakthrough. When it comes to making a choice between embracing what we have experienced as a stepping-stone to a higher way of being or numbing ourselves to our thoughts and feelings and living in a permanent state of self-righteous suffering, many people still vote to sleepwalk. At the end of the day, the only thing that has put many of us on the healing path was the final awareness that if *we* didn't change, *nothing else* would change.

Are you at that point yet? Do you know that you are the thing that must change if you want to have different and better experiences in your life? Think of it this way: the experiences you are having right now, in every aspect of your life, are mirror reflections of your dominant negative thought patterns. Wherever you sense darkness, pain, confusion, or suffering, that's an area in which a pattern of thinking is being reflected back to you. If things are not as you would have them be in a certain area of your life— whether it's relationships, finances, career, health, or self-satisfaction—a mental file is blocking the light from that area of your soul. Have you acknowledged that it's possible for you to block your own goodness and greatness? Are you aware of your blocks? Can you accept that you, consciously or unconsciously, have caused your own pain and suffering? And are you finally willing to act—to employ a new method for getting out of your own way?

I invite you to avoid the temptation to receive these inquiries as a form of blame or self-condemnation. Instead, recognize from all you have read thus far that getting stuck in the negative aspects of life is a very common human experience because of the way we are taught to use the power of our minds. As children, we do what we are told, and we mimic what we see. Our education system teaches us to memorize and repeat what others have said and done, placing the opinion of others above our own intuitive sense of what is good and right for our own authentic self-expression. In the world around us, in order to be accepted and validated, we are expected to toe the lines that others have created. Our successes and accomplishments are measured by what others think and say about who we are and what we have or have not done. Throughout the process of living, growing, learning, and doing, we often lose sight of what it means to be human in loving and authentic ways.

Getting over anything—whether it's a broken relationship or a childhood trauma—begins with a thought. Getting through what you desire to get through requires committed and consistent action. That's the truth of thought therapy. The thought therapy process is not a magic bullet. It's a self-honoring, self-supportive, self-loving way of tapping into the power of your greatest asset: your mind. It's a process for reclaiming your identity and using it to the best of your ability to eliminate personal suffering, restriction, and limitation at all levels of your being.

As the legendary Rev. Dr. Johnnie Colemon, founder of Chicago's Christ Universal Temple and the Universal Foundation for Better Living, taught her students:

> You are the thinker that thinks the thought that makes the thing. . . . Everything begins in the mind. And, if it begins in the mind, whatever the effects are in your world, life and affairs, you must find the cause. There's a cause for every effect. You've got to think the right thoughts because every thought comes back to you. Whatever you think, you have made it.

Today, more than ever before, it's time to do this work. Too many of us have been led astray, disappointed, let down, and, in the worst-case scenarios, betrayed by the "do this, get that" systems of the world. On the other hand, way too many of us are stuck wondering why it seems that the more we do, the less we get or have in our lives. May I offer—this is not that! This is not about doing something in order to get anything. This work is not a bargaining system. The GOI thought therapy process, and the supporting prayers and affirmations, is about being and becoming the truth of who you are. It's about transformation—doing the work required to achieve your desired results.

This very sacred work is about transforming your thoughts and your attitudes about your thoughts in order to become a productive cocreator with the Source and Creator of your life. Think of it this way: you get to choose. You can be a 40-watt bulb, barely glowing, trying to find your way through repetitive chaos, crisis, and confusion, or you can be a lighthouse, radiating waves of brilliant light that will guide you and others to safer, calmer, more loving, and gentler shores. You can stay tangled in the mess of wires and filaments that you either inherited or picked up then filed away, or you can untangle and unhook yourself from what has always been so that you can align yourself with the possibilities of what you can create with the right thoughts. The choice, Beloved, is yours. It's time to do your thought therapy work because, to quote Dr. Colemon's lifelong mantra, *"It works if you work it!"* I will meet you in the file room.

BLESSINGS
AND GRATITUDE

✦

*T*here are simply no words that can adequately express the depths of my gratitude for the life I have been graced to live as a woman, mother, teacher, minister, and student. I never would have made it this far without God's grace, mercy, and love. And because of God's love, I have been loved and supported by a countless number of incredible people. I call them my angels.

The loving support of those angels is the reason you are holding this book in your hands. Among them—first and foremost—is my editor and wordsmith, Cheryl Woodruff: you have been the wind *and* my wings on this one. I thank you. Almasi Wilcots and Helen Jones: there simply are no words. Ms. Gina Marshall, my rainmaker: thank you for giving me a reason to buy a new umbrella! Ms. Kristine Mills: I cannot believe that I have never laid eyes on you, and you still got it all done brilliantly. Ms. Nora Reichard, our extraordinary line-by-line master, who, though tempted, never gave up on us. Ms. Cindy Shaw, for yet another beautiful interior design. Ms. Kirsten Melvey, a.k.a. my assistant: you are my calm in the storm. Sir Rodney Scott, my manager, driver, social secretary, and gatekeeper: you are simply the best. Kenneth Browning, my attorney and friend of 25-plus years: without you, none of this would have been birthed. Julie Groome, who has mastered the art of hunting me down when Ken Browning is looking for me. Angie Lile, my social media postmaster, and her team. Reid Tracy and the Hay House family, with a special shout out to Perry Crowe, Richelle Fredson, and Nicolette Young, for always, and in all ways, being willing to support me as well as the work I do.

The Inner Visions Institute family, whose prayers have lifted me higher: Rev. Carmen Gonzalez, Rev. Olubumi Irene Robinson, Rev. Lydia Ruiz, Rev. Tammy Manly, Rev. Elease Welch, Rev. Nancy Yeates, Rev. Pamela Bryant, Rev. Karen Burns, Rev. JoAnne Lee, Rev. Yawo Heather Mizell, Rev. Rosetta Hillary, Rev. Amina Christine Pierra, Rev. Candas Ifama Barnes, Rev. Matt Cartwright, Rev. Lynn Barber, Rev. Peter Ripley, Rev. Yolanda, Rev. Patty Hamilton; coaches Jackie Smith, Robert Pruitt, Althea Danzey, Ershell Williams, Maqueita Eleazer, Monica Bergandi; and all of my IVISD students.

The Inner Visions "God Squad," my workshop team, which includes many of those above as well as Iya Yawfah Shakor, Danni Stillwell, Janet Barber, Charlotte Wilson, Deanna Matthias, and Sydney Beasley.

I owe my sanity to my BFF and sister-friend for life, Rev. Shaheerah Stephens; to my Prayer Mother, Raina Bundy, and to my godfather, Professor Ochun Kunle Erindele. My godchildren, members of Ile Omi Meji, who never lose faith in me: Aldo Valmon Clarke, Ronald King-Shepherd, Adegbola Nobles, Dr. Akmal Muwwakil, Kimberly Perry, Rev. LaTonya Taylor, LaToya Smith, Marcy Francis, Seshmi Carol Small, and Zakiya Fatin.

I owe the life of my vision, my dream come true, to Oprah Winfrey, my sister-woman; Jon Sinclair, my co-executive producer on *Iyanla Fix My Life*; and Paul Harrison and the technical Dream Team Red: Champ, Rodney, Monroe, and Mr. George. Sheka; I did not forget you, or you, Min. Laura Rawlings, Dr. Dinorah Nieves, and Eduardo Read.

Finally, to my children, who have given me permission to mother in the world without ever complaining: Damon Bware Vanzant, his wife ChaVon Kells-Vanzant, and Yawo Nisa Vanzant, thank you for allowing me to be who I am.

To you all, I lift my voice with praise and thanksgiving.

To God be the glory!

ABOUT THE AUTHOR

✦

*I*yanla Vanzant is one of the country's most celebrated writers and public speakers, and she's among the most influential, socially engaged, and acclaimed spiritual life coaches of our time. Host and executive producer of the award-winning hit *Iyanla: Fix My Life* on OWN: Oprah Winfrey Network, Iyanla's focus on faith,  empowerment, and loving relationships has inspired millions around the world. A woman of passion, vision, and purpose, Iyanla is also the cofounder and executive director of Inner Visions Institute for Spiritual Development.

To receive a free subscription to Iyanla's newsletter, please register at www.Iyanla.com.

INNER VISIONS INSTITUTE FOR SPIRITUAL DEVELOPMENT

*Where the Mind Meets the Heart and
the Soul Remembers Its Purpose*

Join Iyanla for

Online and In-Person

Classes, Workshops, and Seminars

Coaches Training

Ministerial Ordination

For More Information Visit Us At:
InnerVisionsWorldwide.com

Titles of Related Interest

FORGIVENESS: 21 Days to Forgive Everyone for Everything
By Iyanla Vanzant

IF YOU CAN SEE IT, YOU CAN BE IT:
12 Street Smart Lessons for Success
By Chef Jeff Henderson

ALMOST WHITE: Forced Confessions of a Latino in Hollywood
By Rick Najera

HEALTH FIRST: The Black Women's Wellness Guide
By Eleanor Hinton Hoytt and Hilary Beard

PEACE FROM BROKEN PIECES:
How to Get Through What You're Going Through
By Iyanla Vanzant

BRAINWASHED: Challenging the Myth of Black Inferiority
By Tom Burrell

All of the above are available at your local bookstore, or
may be ordered by contacting Hay House (see next page).

We hope you enjoyed this Hay House book. If you'd like to receive our online catalog featuring additional information on Hay House books and products, or if you'd like to find out more about the Hay Foundation, please contact:

Hay House, Inc., P.O. Box 5100, Carlsbad, CA 92018-5100
(760) 431-7695 or (800) 654-5126
(760) 431-6948 (fax) or (800) 650-5115 (fax)
www.hayhouse.com® • www.hayfoundation.org

———

Published and distributed in Australia by:
Hay House Australia Pty. Ltd., 18/36 Ralph St., Alexandria NSW 2015
Phone: 612-9669-4299 • *Fax:* 612-9669-4144 • www.hayhouse.com.au

Published and distributed in the United Kingdom by:
Hay House UK, Ltd., Astley House, 33 Notting Hill Gate, London W11 3JQ
Phone: 44-20-3675-2450 • *Fax:* 44-20-3675-2451 • www.hayhouse.co.uk

Published in India by: Hay House Publishers India,
Muskaan Complex, Plot No. 3, B-2, Vasant Kunj, New Delhi 110 070
Phone: 91-11-4176-1620 • *Fax:* 91-11-4176-1630 • www.hayhouse.co.in

Distributed in Canada by:
Raincoast Books, 2440 Viking Way, Richmond, B.C. V6V 1N2
Phone: 1-800-663-5714 • *Fax:* 1-800-565-3770 • www.raincoast.com

———

Access New Knowledge.
Anytime. Anywhere.

Learn and evolve at your own pace
with the world's leading experts.

www.hayhouseU.com